# DEEP & WILD

# DEEP & WILD

On Mountains, Opossums & Finding Your Way
in West Virginia

LAURA JACKSON

AUTUMN
HOUSE PRESS
Pittsburgh, PA

Published by Autumn House Press
All Rights Reserved

*Deep & Wild: On Mountains, Opossums & Finding Your Way in West Virginia*
Copyright © 2024 by Laura Jackson
ISBN: 9781637680988

Book and Cover Design by Kinsley Stocum
Author Photo by Heather Kalb

This book is nonfiction. It reflects the author's present recollections of experiences over time. Some names and characteristics have been changed, some events have been compressed, and some dialogue has been recreated.

LIBRARY OF CONGRESS CATALOGING-IN-PUBLICATION DATA
Names: Jackson, Laura, 1979- author.
Title: Deep & wild : on mountains, opossums & finding your way in West
    Virginia / Laura Jackson.
Other titles: Deep and wild
Identifiers: LCCN 2024024339 (print) | LCCN 2024024340 (ebook) | ISBN
    9781637680988 (paperback) | ISBN 9781637680995 (epub)
Subjects: LCSH: Jackson, Laura, 1979- | Appalachians (People)--West
    Virginia--Biography. | Outdoor life--West Virginia. | Natural
    history--West Virginia. | West Virginia--Social life and customs. |
    Appalachians (People)--West Virginia--Social life and customs. |
    Wheeling (W. Va.)--Biography. | BISAC: LITERARY COLLECTIONS / Essays |
    LITERARY COLLECTIONS / American / General
Classification: LCC F245.42.J32 A3 2024  (print) | LCC F245.42.J32  (ebook)
    | DDC 975.4/043092 [B]--dc23/eng/20240603
LC record available at https://lccn.loc.gov/2024024339
LC ebook record available at https://lccn.loc.gov/2024024340

Printed in the United States on acid-free paper that meets the international standards of permanent books intended for purchase by libraries.

Autumn House Press is a nonprofit corporation whose mission is the publication and promotion of poetry and other fine literature. The press gratefully acknowledges support from individual donors, public and private foundations, and government agencies. This book was supported in part by the Pennsylvania Council on the Arts, a state agency funded by the Commonwealth of Pennsylvania.

*For Grandad*

# Table of Contents

## I.

## II.

*Somewhere someone's listening to trees talk in a language like song, a song that's been going on longer than time.*

—Marc Harshman, "Dispatch from the Mountain State"

# To Catch a Craw

en lifted the smooth, flat rock and plunged his hand into the shallows of the Greenbrier River. Water shot out from beneath his palm and the river bottom clouded over as he stirred up silt. The current swirled around our crouching bodies. Often, when my kids pulled out a crawdad, it was attached to their finger, their pink flesh gone white in its vise.

"It pinches but not really but kind of a little bit but just stop being a weenie, Mom," Ben said. I didn't want to. I was a weenie. I'd never caught anything more than river dust, and the craw knew it. They took advantage of my hesitation, every time.

To catch a craw, my sons told me, you really need to commit. They hide under flat rocks, but it's rarely a simple lift-and-catch. When the rock comes up, a billowing cloud of sediment obscures the riverbed and your intended target, and in that moment, they bolt. Craw escape by propelling themselves backward, tails tucked, at astonishing speed. Experienced craw hunters may have a net ready, especially if they can anticipate which direction the animal is going to go, but this is difficult when the silt clouds your view. It takes dexterity and practice.

Crawdad, or crayfish, eat whatever they can find on the river bottom, including dead and decaying plant and animal matter. We have roughly thirty species in West Virginia, both aquatic and burrowing. While some have been extirpated, notable species include the endangered Guyandotte River crayfish (found in only two Wyoming County streams), the Greenbrier Cave crayfish, and a newly discovered, bright blue, burrowing species, the Blue Teays Mudbug. Several species and their habitats are federally protected due to dwindling numbers, a result of habitat destruction, often from coal mining operations.

While scientifically correct, few West Virginians call them crayfish. Unless you've got a PhD, calling them crayfish around here marks you as someone out of place. It's like saying New Or-*leens*, rather than the way my grandparents, born and raised in the Big Easy, always said it: "New *Aw*-linz." Drop crayfish into riverside conversation amidst anglers and, immediately, you're an outsider. Expect your license plate to be examined.

"Did they say 'crayfish'? Damn Virginians. I bet they got Perrier in that cooler, too."

I've got a degree in environmental studies, but I'm a native West Virginian, and I don't want to be an outsider in my home state. Most Appalachians call them crawfish or crawdad. (I know this because I took a very scientific social media poll of my friends—some from northern Appalachia, some from southern Appalachia, and a few Floridians who just wanted to add their twenty-five cents.) But I've never liked either term, as the animal is neither a fish nor a dad. A sperm donor, yes, but the male crawdad aren't out there coaching their spawn through a T-ball game. And forget crawdaddy. I'm not uttering anything that makes me sound like a backwoods porn star. Some folks use the term mudbugs, which is too close to bedbugs for me. So, I've settled on saying craw. Everyone here knows what I'm talking about when I say craw, and nobody feels the need to check my cooler or my academic credentials. And I'm not the only one who favors craw. In my tackle box, I have a lure by the Rebel company shaped like a crayfish. It's called the Wee Craw. They make a bigger version called the Big Craw and a smaller one called the Teeny Wee Craw. Alternatively, if you need a deep diving lure, you can go with the Deep Wee or the Deep Teeny Wee Craw. And if you're feeling especially finite, whip out your Micro Craw. After all, it's not the size of the craw that matters—it's how you dangle it in the water.

Nevertheless, live bait has the advantage of realistic movement and delectable smell. Despite the craw's propensity for mischief, no other bait so tempts a smallmouth bass, which is why the craw hunt continues. The search may be the most entertaining part of a day on the river because there's another crayfish characteristic that becomes glaringly apparent when you do catch one. As you hold the tiny creature up to your face, its legs flail and stretch outward to appear more threatening. Its antennae swirl around, trying to make sense of its position in space. This is an animal on the defense, but only for a second, because the most notable quality of the craw is its supremely shitty attitude. They're the chihuahuas of the rocks, the Napoleons of the river. The craw is the ultimate curmudgeon. It raises its claws and swipes at your face. *Come at me!* I've never seen an animal so tiny yet so determined to kick my ass. The craw doesn't care how small it is or how big you are—it wants to take you down. Craw defense is craw offense.

Of course, holding a shrimpy brawler high in the air while it takes a swing at you with an I'll-kill-you-you-gangly-motherfucker glint in its eye only makes us laugh, which probably incenses it even further. And I had to sympathize with a craw that Ben's brother, Andy, caught on the Greenbrier River that day. Minding its own business one moment and the next, plucked from its home, held aloft, and mocked by giants.

"Look at that guy," I said to Andy. "He wants to murder us." The critter swung its claws ferociously, and in that moment, I was certain I was looking not at a set of pinchers but at a tiny middle finger held aloft in my face. *Screw you, lady! Screw all of you!* We gave the contentious crustacean to my husband, who hooked it through the tail and cast it downstream. It must have been an unforgivable insult. Craw are swift and grumpy and funny-looking, but they hold onto their dignity. As it flew through the air, legs rigid and outstretched, I could almost feel its rage.

Though bass love craw, there's a downside to using them as bait: the animal is obnoxious when hooked. It's a lot like tying your dog to a chair. She wanders in circles, weaves around your legs and the chair's legs and, within twelve seconds, is hopelessly tangled. Then, she just stands there, immobilized and utterly confused as to how it happened. And you try to untangle her and get frustrated and ask her why she does this *every single time* and how hard is it to just lie down and freaking stay there, dog? That's like fishing with a live craw. You can see your line moving as they crawl under rocks, over rocks, around and through logs. You may be tempted to set the hook, thinking a fish has taken a bite. Nope. It's that wretched craw, wandering around the river bottom. It happened to my husband, who reeled in to find the little twerp had doubled back and was crawling toward him along the fishing line like a tightrope walker. Behind the craw, several feet of braided line twisted and wrapped around itself. By the time he untangled the knots, he was frustrated. He recast both line and craw, claws again extended in fury, downriver toward a deep hole. When the animal hit bottom, it apparently decided it had had enough: it removed the hook from its tail and sauntered off, no doubt in a huff.

Not every craw-catcher is scouring the river for bait, though. There are plenty of folks who eat them. My friend Christina grew up in Marshall County, West Virginia, a rural place. She told me about a swanky political fundraiser she attended on Long Island. The hall was decorated in the swag of schmoozing, and the event's visual centerpiece was a canoe filled with boiled crayfish. She found herself staring at the crimson pile of claws and legs. No doubt, memories of her childhood rushed in—hot July days, "crick" shoes sliding along smooth rocks slick with brown algae, mayflies rising, sunburns and shouts and the heavy smell of humidity trapped beneath the summer canopy.

"Aren't you going to have a crayfish?" someone asked her.

Christina looked at the boat, piled high with the familiar lobsterlings. The presentation was meant to feel exotic, a rare and adventurous delicacy brought in from afar.

She squinted and shook her head.

"Where I come from," she said, "we call that bait."

Christina's event is called a craw boil. The tradition belongs to Louisiana, where crawfish are regularly eaten, and the culmination is the presentation of craw not on a plate or in a chafing dish but in a towering heap. After boiling them, you chuck them on the table in a steaming mound, sprinkle on your seasoning of choice, toss in a few ears of corn and, perhaps, a mix of andouille sausage, garlic cloves, or whatever pleases your palate. Boil-goers pluck craw from the pile.

A mess of craw is just that—a mess. They need to be cleaned of mud before they can be cooked, and you can buy an eighty-dollar crawfish washer if you're so inclined. It functions like a jetted tub: a hose attaches to the base of the bucket and the water shoots out at an angle, creating a current that stirs the craw and scrubs the mud off. After ten or fifteen minutes, when the water runs clear, the craw are ready for another sort of hot tub.

This is where I get uncomfortable because, until this step, the stars of the craw boil are usually very much alive.

I watched a YouTube video on how to boil craw and spent most of it dreading the moment when ten pounds of live crustaceans would go into the seething, orange stew. The hosts of the video, enthusiastic bar-beque chefs, spoke of the craw as though they were potatoes or carrots. The animals crawled all over each other in a mesh bag that twitched with their movements. When the time came, the hosts made a Jacuzzi joke and dropped them in, as one would a donut into a fryer.

I'm not sure how to justify my discomfort. It's incredibly hypocritical of me to sit here feeling upset about the boiling of crustaceans when I had a pulled pork sandwich for dinner last night. Nobody wants animals to suffer, but it's much easier to push this conflict away when your din-ner arrives having already shuffled off its mortal coil.

"Well, it's already dead here on my plate. Can't let it go to waste. Ethical dilemmas are more of a lunch discussion anyway. Oh, there's bacon, too? Shit, pass it over." Maybe these feelings boil down to the moment you meet your dinner for the first time. Dead dinner, enjoyable. Live dinner, disturbing. And watching that bag of craw shimmy on You-Tube disturbed me.

I'm not the only one. In 2003, David Foster Wallace visited the annual Maine Lobster Festival for *Gourmet Magazine* and came away unsettled about the nature of the festival and the consumption of the crustaceans in general. While festivalgoers are tying on their plastic bibs and lining up to partake in the celebration, he wrote, the lobsters in the mess tent are huddled in their temporary tanks, looking stressed, and when they go into the pot, it looks like a painful death.

It must take a certain constitution to be the boiler, to stand there all day, listening to them clang desperately on the pot lid. To paraphrase Wallace, lobsters *really* hate being boiled alive. And maybe these sea-food festivals are unique, because I can't think of a whole lot of other American events where the main course is slaughtered while folks are standing in line to eat it. We like our food dead. We don't want blood on our hands. And I have to wonder if the Maine Lobster Festival would be as popular if you had to boil your own lobster. Pluck him from his tank, stare him down, chuck him in, and listen to that screaming sound they make, even if it is just steam escaping the animal's carapace.

I've never eaten a craw. I'd like to know what they taste like, sort of. Craw can't bang on the pot's lid, but I don't have the stomach to plunk a mass of them into a pot of boiling water for the sake of a crayfish essay. Admittedly, at the end of the how-to video on YouTube, when the barbeque chefs dumped the scarlet, steaming mudbugs out onto a cutting board, they looked like they smelled pretty good. But it was a twice-removed sensory experience, so don't base your next backyard gathering on what I've written, here.

"Time to eat these guys," one of the YouTube chefs said. He picked up a craw, broke it in two, placed the upper half of the animal's body against his lips, and sucked audibly.

"All the juice is in the head," he said. The other guy did the same thing and made a slurping noise as his cheeks pulled in with the force of his suck.

At this point in my research, Ben looked over my shoulder.

"Is he sucking that craw's brains out?" he asked.

The chefs demonstrated how to break the exoskeleton and eat the tail meat. But by then, they'd lost me. The brain-suck was enough to turn me off. And, like Christina said, it still looked like the contents of an upended tackle box, anyway.

The craw in a craw boil are *Procambarus clarkii*, the Louisiana crawfish. According to the West Virginia Reddit community, *our* endemic species taste like mud, though it doesn't stop locals from considering a feast now and then.

"Where can you buy live crawfish for a crawfish boil?" someone asked on a regional thread, hoping for a hookup with a seafood shack or fishmonger.

"They're free in the creek," came the reply.

We never once thought about tasting the Greenbrier River craw the kids caught. I may abhor the name "mudbugs," but that's what they look like. It's easy to see how the craw wash is such an important step in the boiling process. Still, even if our craw looked clean and delectable, I'm not sure I'm ready to suck anything's freshly cooked brains out. I'm not even brave enough to grab one out from under a rock.

By the end of our weekend on the Greenbrier River, I still hadn't caught a craw. The kids had a difficult time disguising their pity for their poor mom. She fell a lot, they noted, and wasn't fast enough. Also, she was clearly afraid of being pinched, an anxiety that compounded when Ben found and suffered the wrath of a hellgrammite, the larval stage of a horrifying creature known as a dobsonfly. If you're unfamiliar with that insect, imagine an earwig had a threesome with a dragonfly and a rhinoceros beetle. Larvae look like a Jurassic throwback: dark bodies, spindly legs, and piercing mandibles that rival the craw's claws in size. The difference between a hellgrammite and a craw is that the craw pinches you to teach you some respect; the hellgrammite does it just to be a dick.

After one too many hesitations when I should have been bold and stuck my hand under a rock, my family eased up on their expectations. It was obvious to them I wasn't getting the hang of the hunt. And though they didn't say it, I knew I was the outsider. To be fair, I'd *helped* to catch several. I was good at spotting which way the craw darted when the boys lifted the rocks, so they made me The Official Craw Spotter, but I was pretty sure it was the kind of consolation job you give the loser of the group, the one who has poor hand-eye coordination and little chance of success on her own. Still, I'd rather be pitied than pinched, a thing I have yet to experience. It seems like an unavoidable part of this riverside ritual and a necessary step in the education of a competent crawcatcher, and I know, beyond a shadow of a doubt, that I am indeed being a weenie. I guess I don't want the craw badly enough. Maybe craw-hunting isn't for everybody, regardless of where they're born. Maybe, when all is said and done, I'm grabbing at something I'm not meant to catch.

# Being West Virginian

I wonder if there's a state more misunderstood than West Virginia. Unless you've spent time here, you may only know we're an oddly shaped plot of land sandwiched between the East Coast, Midwest, and South. While West Virginia's outline is unforgettable, the land within its recognizable borders may be a mystery. People unfamiliar with our state are often confused—are we coal miners? Are we shoeless hillbillies? Are we all banjo-playing, moonshine-guzzling mountain folk in worn overalls with bathtubs in our kitchens?

No. And yes. Some of us are and do, but a lot of us aren't and don't. Being West Virginian is full of contradictions. For example, we're home to the Green Bank Telescope, the world's largest fully steerable radio telescope that's been instrumental in making remarkable discoveries from deep space. We're also legally allowed to eat roadkill.

Plenty of what you hear is true. We're coal country, a place where miners unionized and went to war with the coal companies. We were part of the Hatfield-McCoy feud (we were the Hatfields), and we separated from Virginia in 1863 because we didn't like the way the South did things. We're a longtime blue state turned red in recent years. We're mountain country—you've heard John Denver's song. And when the West Virginia Mountaineers win football games, the students of West Virginia University have been known to set their couches ablaze on the sidewalks of Morgantown in drunken celebration.

As for the moonshine, it's not ubiquitous. But everyone knows someone who makes it at home, flavored with strawberry or apple pie or key lime. It shows up at parties and gatherings in Mason jars, and I may or may not have witnessed it being subtly purchased in the elementary school pickup line. There's no guzzling, though—that's a good way to burn a hole in your esophagus.

And for the record, Californians are legally allowed to eat roadkill, too. (Pro tip: it goes down easier with a swig of White Lightning.)

As for the stereotypes, it shouldn't need to be said that we don't marry our cousins. (That's low-hanging fruit, and we're going to be disappointed if it's the best you can come up with.) Nor does banjo music float ominously through the hollows. Unless, of course, someone is playing the banjo. In a hollow. It happens.

For every person I've met in the world who truly knows West Virginia, there are two more who have nothing to go on beyond a comedic portrayal. These classic caricatures are outdated to the point of absurdity, yet they persist, perhaps because stereotypes are born from a seed of truth. Without a doubt, somebody here has flattened a critter with their Chevy and fried it in a pan. You're more likely to find a four-wheeler than a Wi-Fi router in a few counties. And somewhere in the far corners of Roane County, a shotgun-wielding grandma just dropped a ten-point buck from the window beside her kitchen tub.

Many West Virginians own this with pride, while others feel conflicted and try to both excuse and explain us to the rest of the country, to prove our worth. We're compelled, by some odd mix of shame and pride, to not only claim this land as our home, but also to justify why we've chosen to be *of* this place. West Virginia is inconsistency. It's beauty and misery, freedom and addiction, devotion and resentment. It's people who worship nature and people who tear it apart. Rock climbers and gas drillers. Organic epicures and Mountain Dew swillers. Teetotalers and wine snobs. Pig farmers and pot farmers. There's a lot to dissect, so if you want to unpack West Virginia's complexities, come on over. We can sit down with a jar of pawpaw hooch and watch the lightning bugs while we dig into socioeconomics and cultural norms and, eventually, fall over backward off the deck.

Also, the human element is only one part of the equation. There are two West Virginias: the human and the wild. While the former offers an endless loop of joy and pain, the land itself reaches deep into your gut. Our mountains are old. Geologists say the Appalachians were once among the mightiest, most foreboding ranges on Earth, but eons of existence have worn them down to a gentler form. It's easy to mistake their rounded curves for mildness, to rank them low on the list of impressive ranges, far beneath the Sierras or Rockies. But West Virginia has seen things the jagged peaks of the West can only imagine in their infant dreams. When you travel through our mountains, they wipe clean the notions you've accumulated about banjos and bathtubs. It's a landscape of age and wisdom. Of contentment. We know that quiet intensity. It's woven through us like the tendrils of an ancient nervous system.

My god, we love this land.

We're not shy about showing it, either. I've never seen state pride on display more than it is here. Go to the store and you're guaranteed to see someone wearing a cap with West Virginia University's famous flying WV logo, someone with a Monongahela National Forest sticker on their car, or a jacket with the state's distinctive profile emblazoned on the fabric. You'll see West Virginia tattoos, WVU bandannas, and kitschy tees depicting something unique and distinctly West Virginian, like a pepperoni roll or a giant hellbender salamander. These trappings express our love for this place, but when we're out of state, they're also a bright, shining beacon. It's how we find other West Virginians in the world, even if they're expats. We'll be drawn to each other, like magnetic north, outed by our ball caps or T-shirts or license plates. We'll put aside whatever we're doing or wherever we're going for a moment and stand in the Old Faithful parking lot in Yellowstone or on the beach in the Galápagos Islands and talk about home.

"Where you from?"

"Upshur County. Where you from?"

"Hampshire County."

"My brother's in Hampshire County."

"Is that right? My brother's in Wyoming County."

"I went to a church retreat in Wyoming County last spring."

"Really? My daughter's a preacher in Pocahontas County."

"I love Pocahontas County."

With fifty-five counties, this can go on for a while, but our county of residence is how we identify ourselves. Two-thirds of West Virginians live in a rural area—Monroe County still has no traffic lights. Some unincorporated communities are little more than an intersection and a gas station. So, while almost nobody knows Smoot, West Virginia (except for the Smootians), everyone knows Greenbrier County. Geographic generalizations work for us.

The irony of meeting a familiar face far from home is that, while we're so excited to be out of state and seeing something new, the sight of another West Virginian strikes the sweetest note. We've found someone in this wide world who understands what we're so unable to convey to residents of the other forty nine states. We don't have to explain, "Yes, we're from West Virginia, and yes, we have all our teeth and running water, and no, we aren't coal miners, but yes, we know plenty, and yes, it *is* a beautiful state." We meet each other and grasp hands and find, suddenly, more joy in our bond than we do in the vacation we took to get away from the place that connects us. It's comforting to encounter our own, because when we meet people from other places, there's a checklist of corrections we have to run through regarding our existence, and the primary topic is often geography. The conversations, vastly different from the ones we have with our Mountain State brethren, inevitably go like this:

"Where are you from?"

"Arizona. You?"

"West Virginia."

"West Virginia! Hey, I have a cousin in Richmond. James Leonard. Sells insurance. You know him?"

It's *always* Richmond. I don't know what it is about Richmond, Virginia, that is attracting your cousins, but it must really be something if they've all decided to settle there.

At this point in the conversation, the West Virginian has two choices. If we're young and proud, we'll try to educate the new acquaintance on the intricacies of geography (Richmond is about two hundred miles from the West Virginia border) and the Civil War. We may do it sincerely or sarcastically, depending on how many times we've had this conversation.

"Actually, I don't know if you've heard, but West Virginia seceded from Virginia a while ago. It was kind of a big deal. There was a war."

Even worse, some people call us "western Virginia," like we're some scrawny limb that wasn't amputated all the way and is now just hanging out there, waving people through Monroe County intersections because there aren't any red lights.

Older West Virginians will have heard the cousin-in-Richmond quip many times. With age comes wisdom and patience, so their response will usually be, "Yes, Richmond is lovely," or "How nice for your cousin." They've lived a life of being misunderstood and misrepresented. They've seen maps on TV that leave West Virginia off entirely because some graphic designer failed third-grade geography. There on the screen is Ohio, snuggled up to Pennsylvania and Virginia. I saw a fifty-state ice cube tray for sale on Amazon. Well, forty-nine states, because West Virginia was gone, wiped from existence. We're a uniquely shaped state—hard to forget, you'd think—but it happens a lot. However, as we age, these mistakes cease to surprise us, and the blessing of this land is that it teaches us to flow rather than fight. We can only change the perception of our state one ice cube tray at a time.

We work hard at that. Over the years, I've introduced many out-of-staters to West Virginia's beauty and history, but it hasn't always been a smooth process. Some people are more open-minded than others, and I learned this when I went to college in St. Petersburg, Florida. My college boyfriend made West Virginia jokes a religion. A New Yorker by birth, he knew West Virginia as little more than a collection of stereotypes and took enormous pleasure in teasing me. He joked about missing teeth and kissing cousins and often wondered how many tractors he might see on the interstate if he visited me. I spent our two-year relationship trying to prove I was as competent as any New Yorker but never succeeded.

He and I had many adventures. One notable afternoon, we hopped in my car with my roommate and headed east, into the interior of Florida where, every spring, Plant City hosts the annual Florida Strawberry Festival. (In West Virginia, we celebrate the Buckwheat Festival, the Ramps and Rail Festival, the Mothman Festival, Trout Fest, Carp Fest, and, indeed, the Roadkill Cook-off, to name but a few.) Plant City's yearly event focuses on strawberries in any form, be it jam, jelly, shortcake, ice cream, or bread. You'll also find the stomach-churning rides that spin around in a circle and occasionally toss riders like fructose-infused hacky sacks.

As we filtered out of the St. Pete/Tampa area and turned east toward Plant City, the traffic thinned. I set the cruise control and settled back into my seat. Behind me, someone blared their horn. I jumped. It wasn't a long, angry note but a manic series of honks. *Beep! Beep! Beep beep beep be-be-be-be-beeeeeep!*

"Jesus," my boyfriend said.

I peered into the rearview mirror.

"Yeah," I said. "What the hell?"

The honking from behind escalated into a solid, frenzied howl as the driver closed the distance between us at alarming speed.

"This guy is psychotic," I said. "I'm getting over." I shifted into the slow lane to let the lunatic pass me. I hoped he'd zip by and vanish into the eastern horizon. But as the vehicle—an old beater of a truck with peeling paint and mismatched tires—approached mine, the driver let off the gas to maintain an even pace with me. Two young men in faded ball caps sat in the cab, and as they pulled up beside my car, they began to holler and scream at me. The guy on the passenger side leaned his entire torso out the window, but his expression wasn't furious. It was exultant.

"Heeey!" he shouted. "Haaaaaayyy! Whoohooooo!" The driver, too, grinned at me with an expression of recognition. His whole arm waggled back and forth in a hysterical wave. I gave them a look I hoped would both acknowledge their presence and discourage them from any further contact and slowed down to let them speed by to whatever crackpot convention they were attending.

"That's creepy," my roommate said.

"They look like they just crawled out of the woods," my boyfriend said.

As the truck accelerated, the man in the passenger seat tucked his body back into the cab with a final wave.

"Idiots like that have no business behind the wheel of a three-thousand-pound machine," I said.

And then, as those idiots pulled away, I saw their license plate, accented with blue and gold. I saw the phrase printed along its bottom: *Wild, Wonderful.*

West Virginia.

Like magnetic north, my people had found me and were obligated not only to acknowledge our sameness in a faraway place, but also to reach out. To literally reach out—the guy had nearly eaten pavement to grab my attention.

I held my breath, waiting for my passengers to see what I'd seen, and when they did, my boyfriend's laugh exploded out of his chest.

He cackled until he bit his lip, and for the rest of our relationship, he returned again and again to that moment to argue for the truth in West Virginia's stereotypes. No matter how many brilliant West Virginians he might meet, those two friendly, simple souls would always fit precisely into the hillbilly trope he was so fond of.

My cheeks flushed at his state-shaming. And I had been mortified by those men's behavior on such a dangerous road. But that license plate, speeding away, was indeed a beacon. I didn't admit it, but it brought me more joy than any strawberry could. There was no way to explain to my friends the connection I had with those odd but merry travelers in the truck, and I never bothered to. West Virginia had come to find me.

Two decades later, I took a workshop with the writer Paul Hertneky, author of *Rust Belt Boy*. He writes about food and travel and growing up in a Pittsburgh mill town. My home state came up again and again in the writing prompts.

"You could write about West Virginia," Paul mused. "But you have to figure out what West Virginia is really good at, something no other state can claim." I sat with that statement overnight. I sat with it for a week. For a year. And every time I came up with a piece or a place that made my heart sing, I realized another state was doing it better. Colorado has taller mountains, Arizona has a deeper canyon. Utah has better snow and Vermont, more fall color.

The more I write about West Virginia, the more I think about Paul's query. I've yet to reach a clear answer on exactly what it is we do so well here, what we can claim as our own. I can feel it, of course—we all can. But the words get lost in the translation from emotion to paragraph. What I return to, again and again, is the green earth that rises above us and the water that carves its way down. West Virginia's greatest assets are its deep and wild places, those left behind and off the map. This place is old. With age comes contentment; with contentment comes peace. What West Virginia does best it's been doing for eons: waiting quietly, wearing down, wrapping rough places in forest and smoothing them with stream.

When I'm lacking words, I turn to those whose works have meant so much to me. Breece D'J Pancake was a West Virginia writer known only for a thin volume of short stories published after his suicide in

1979. He would have rocked the literary world—and his home state—had he lived. Kurt Vonnegut said Pancake was the best and most sincere writer he had ever read. Joyce Carol Oates compared his extraordinary gifts to Hemingway's. Pancake wove rural hardship and environmental degradation together with the unique sense of place felt so strongly by Appalachians. It's a sense that's hard to convey to those who don't feel it. Perhaps it's why I can't find the words I'm looking for.

Breece D'J Pancake found them, though.

"I'm going to come back to West Virginia when this is over," he wrote to his mother from Charlottesville before he died. "There's something ancient and deeply-rooted in my soul. I like to think that I have left my ghost up one of those hollows, and I'll never really be able to leave for good until I find it. And I don't want to look for it, because I might find it and have to leave."

We can drift away from this place, but the strongest roots go deep. If Pancake's ghost still haunts the hollows, it's not alone. We're forever attached.

It's what it means to be West Virginian.

# Ain't No Copperhead

L ast weekend at the family cabin, I was sitting on the pontoon boat when some neighbors paddled by on their kayaks.

"Did you see the copperheads?" the man called.

"What?" I asked.

His wife laid her paddle across her lap. "There were two copperheads on your rocks last weekend," she said. "One was absolutely huge."

Her husband took over. "I called the conservancy about it. Ever since they put this riprap on the shoreline, the copperheads have moved in. It's terrible."

I smiled and nodded, knowing the snakes that live in the rocks on the shoreline aren't copperheads—they're northern water snakes, and they have always been present. I'd had this conversation before with other neighbors. Sometimes, the offending snakes were accused of being water moccasins, which live nowhere near West Virginia.

But I didn't bother to mention any of this to my kayaking friends. People really want to report a copperhead, and they get annoyed when you point out that what they've just seen is an "ordinary" snake. For the snakes, I suppose it's like being mistaken for a celebrity. On the one hand, it's great to be treated with fear and awe. On the other, how hurtful to know, deep down, that you're never going to be enough simply because you lack venom. Sometimes I talk to the water snakes.

"You're perfect just the way you are. Keep eating those fish and frogs. You're doing a great job." Not that it matters because these particular serpents are aggressive and cantankerous. They're the grumpy old men of the snake world, chasing you off their lawn and cursing to themselves as they slide into the safety of the rocks.

Wherever they occur, snake sightings can be divisive. Many people let out a shout and back away, but I think most of us are content to let the snakes do what they do on their side of the yard. Often, that's eating rodents, and we're all in favor of that, aren't we? We certainly should be. Then, you've got your snake picker-uppers. While others are retreating at an exponentially increasing velocity—accompanied by vocalizations roughly equivalent to the sound a rabbit makes when it's being mangled by the neighbor's German shepherd—their hands are out and their faces are beaming. These folks know how to handle a wild snake. I do not, but it appears to involve grabbing the animal just behind its head so it cannot whip around and bite. I always wonder how you then put the snake down once it's angry and feeling thrashy. Because I can imagine a scenario in which you're kind of just stuck holding a raging reptile for the long haul. He's part of your world, now. He comes with you on dates. On job interviews.

"This guy? Yeah, I picked him up a few months ago on the Greenbrier River Trail. Mad? Oh, you bet he was. Look at him—he's still mad. I haven't figured out how to put him down yet. Yes, I'd love a cup of coffee, thanks. My hands are kinda full. Can I get a straw with that?"

I'm probably overthinking it.

If snakes had middle fingers, they'd be up at us all the time. Even when we're calm, we're still rousting them from their snoozy places in the sunshine. You can almost see the irritation as they uncoil and slither away in disgust.

*God dammit, here comes that idiot gardener again. Christ, I just got comfortable, and my core temperature hasn't even reached seventy degrees.*

Well, Mr. Snake, your escape will depend on who you're dealing with. Because, in addition to your snake-grabbers, you've got your snake-haters and snake-fearers. I've found that the latter don't really want them dead, but the former seem to go out of their way to whack them. And this is cruel, unnecessary, and stupid, because that snake is minding its own business, doing what nature intended. Like you, it's trying to put food on the table, raise the kids, and enjoy a little downtime in the sun. Imagine your lazy Sunday in the hammock. A craft brew, a little Bob Marley, a bowl of fresh guac, and then *bam!* Someone shows up and beans you in the head with a spade. If you have any sort of striping or patches, you'll be labeled a copperhead. A menace. And before you're dispatched, you'll be told why you're being dispatched.

"You, sir, are a copperhead."

"Uh, no, I'm not. I'm a garter snake."

"Nice try, copperhead. Eat shovel!"

The overreactors do so with gusto. My mother is terrified of snakes. I know this and can empathize, as I am no fan of sizable hirsute arachnids. Anything that looks like it might be able to touch both sides of my neck at the same time is not a creature I want to interact with on a personal level. I also admit to being jumpy around snakes. If you look through my Google photos, you'll find a handful of videos I've taken of them. The clips always begin the same way: The camera jerks around, flashing between my walking feet and a sleepy snake curled up on a rock or bit of warm pavement. You hear my hopeful voice say, "Hellooo, snake." The snake uncoils and zips away to the tune of my shriek, which lands somewhere around a high B. I want to be cool, but I'm nervous.

I guess my kayaking neighbors on the lake that day were in the same chickenshit boat, so I returned to the cabin the following weekend with reassuring news for them.

"I talked to a biologist friend of mine," I said. "He said it's not a copperhead. It's a northern water snake. Not venomous." The only true part of that statement was the identification of the water snake and its harmless nature. I did not talk to a biologist. My source was forty-three years of water snake familiarity. And Google.

There are twenty-three snake species in West Virginia and only two are venomous: the copperhead and the timber rattler. Most descriptions refer to both species as generally more docile than other vipers. Per the Division of Natural Resources, nobody has died from a venomous snakebite in over thirty years, and before that, only four since the 1930s. In over one-half of venomous snakebites, no venom is injected. So I guess copperheads are a lot like most of us: full of empty threats. It's like when I announce my intention to take away Ben's video games if he doesn't stop free-soloing his Ikea dresser. Both of us know I'm not going to do it, because the punishment is too much effort for me and it's easier to puff up and threaten him than to follow through. (This is probably why I've received two separate phone calls about Ben "accidentally" pulling the sink off the wall at summer camp.)

No matter what species they're looking at, people absolutely love to report a venomous snake sighting. It's a badge of honor if you've come across one of West Virginia's two species. The spotter usually has no idea what they've actually seen, and thanks to the fallacy of memory, their mind has created details that may never have existed, but people are downright gleeful when they report a snake. Last summer, my husband and I took the kids to the high mountains of Pendleton County. We own eight acres just outside the one-stoplight town of Franklin. There's nothing on our land but trees, rocks, and, according to reports, a sizable timber rattler.

Timber rattlesnakes come in two phases: yellow and black. Both are banded with chevron-shaped bars ending in a dark tail tipped with a rattle. Like all rattlesnakes, they're thick (my kids would say chonky), and while they may grow to five feet, most are smaller. They're found in the forested mountains of eastern West Virginia, and they're often despised, despite their useful rodent control. You're more likely to be struck by lightning than bitten by a timber rattlesnake.

We visit our acreage once a year. It takes almost five hours to get there from our home in Wheeling, and when we arrive, we stand in the grass, inhale the scent of the pines, and stare at the distant summit of Spruce Knob, West Virginia's highest place, dreaming of the day when we can retreat quietly into the mountains to spend our days hiking and trout fishing. We have a neighbor or two, of course, because we're not the only ones who appreciate a country lifestyle in the Ridge-and-Valley Province of Appalachia.

On a recent visit, we pulled up to the land with the kids and got out. They disappeared into the grass while I inspected our trees. Our neighbor rolled up on his lawn tractor, and it wasn't long before he mentioned that someone had been walking on the top of our little mountain. ("Little" is a relative term. At 2,700-ish feet in elevation, it's small by Pendleton County standards, where West Virginia's tallest ridges dwell. But ours would hold its own among the mountains in the southern part of the state.) The walker reported to our neighbor that he had spotted a monstrous timber rattlesnake. The news filtered from hiker to neighbor to us in the tone of an excited kid who wants to be the first to tattle on his brother.

"So watch them boys out there in the grass," our neighbor warned. I didn't buy it.

The timber rattlesnake's Latin name is *Crotalus horridus*. Horrid rattler. Or, depending on your Greek translation, "horrid castanet."

Horrid? While a notable portion of the population might find rattle-snakes to be horrid creatures, the timber rattler is notoriously shy. We encountered one on the way to the top of Dolly Sods Wilderness, a high, rugged plateau on the Allegheny Front. She had been trying to cross the road and a good Samaritan had stopped his car to help the animal get to her destination. When she reached the dusty ditch, she coiled into a tight little ball and tried to make herself invisible. We stopped our own car and got out to inspect her from a respectful distance, and she was the least horrid castanet I've ever had the privilege of meeting.

When it comes to Latin names, the copperhead has a more descrip-tive—and less judgmental—classification: *Agkistrodon contortrix.* "Intri-cate fishhook." Fishhook refers to its curved fangs; intricate describes its dorsal pattern. Common lore suggests that copperheads smell like a cucumber. At Ohiopyle State Park in southwestern Pennsylvania, there's a waterfall called Cucumber Falls, so named because it's said to be a spot favored by the notorious snakes. Supposedly, if you smell cucumber, you're within striking distance of one.

However, there's no science behind this. A sensitive nose might interpret copperhead musk as melony or cucumbery, but this is a sub-jective determination. Like many snakes, the copperhead can release a musk from its scent glands when threatened, but this may also mix in with feces. So I don't know what kind of freaky farmers' markets are selling these funky vegetables, but the scent is more than a molecule or two away from the average green gourd.

No matter what copperheads smell like, it all comes down to brag-ging rights. I hesitate to tie the claims of a giant, venomous snake encounter to the stereotypically male fascination with length and girth . . . but if the codpiece fits, wear it. I think it's probably something a little more primeval, though. "Snake" means fear—memes call them *danger noodles.* We cannot allow ourselves to trust them or even soften our resolve. Maybe, for some, it's the biblical origin story—when something goes wrong, blame a snake. (Or a woman, but that's a different discus-sion.) "I will put enmity between you and the woman," God said to the serpent. And he pretty much did. For others, perhaps it's the unrelat-able physical form. *Where are your arms and legs, my dude? Why don't you blink? Stop sticking your tongue out at me.* Reptiles feel different, which is their appeal for some and their distastefulness for others. Certainly, they lack fur and facial expressions, but when you take bodily appendages out of the equation and add lightning speed and fangs, it's easy to understand why mammal lovers might not know where to start with a snake.

Snake proponents have an uphill battle, the same one that shark fanatics and pitbull fans fight. How do you change public perception, especially when a few aggressive noodles spoil the proverbial pasta primavera? Moreover, it's not the noodles' fault any more than the sharks'. They're just doing what they evolved to do millions of years before humans appeared (and then freaked out, mocked them on the internet, and drew unrealistic cartoon images comparing them to a soggy string of unleavened dough). So when it comes to thawing cold hearts (the human ones, not the reptiles'), if an educational publication fails to educate, then snake lovers have to try a different approach.

One winter weekend, years ago, I landed on a YouTube clip titled "Ain't No Copperhead." It's a music video, and the song is awesomely ridiculous. A group of men—some bearded, some dressed as hoe-wielding farmers and stoic state troopers—dance around in parking garages and vegetable gardens. The video opens with an irritating yet hypnotic noise that one might describe as music, but in actuality sounds more like a Siamese cat ensnared in a set of venetian blinds. A photo of a copperhead flashes on the screen—a coiled, dusky-eyed reptile sunning itself. "This is a copperhead," a caption reads. Then, side by side, two more photos appear: a DeKay's brown snake and a baby black rat snake. "NOT COPPERHEADS," the text screams in a scarlet rage. And we know we're about to get schooled.

The composers are a North Carolina group called Catching Creation, storytellers who love nature, love wildlife, and have a penchant for penning educational earworms that are a perfect potpourri of hip and ridiculous. Dressed like a hillbilly version of the Village People, they throw themselves into their message: that snake you're about to whack is not a copperhead, so leave it alone!

For those about to queue up YouTube, consider yourself warned: the refrain will settle into your brain like a gopher snake in a garbage can. However, it's also a helpful checklist for identifying a copperhead.

*Yellow tail? No. Green tail? No. Diamond head? No. That ain't no copperhead!*

The video's description offers a little insight into the song's origin. Team member Thomas Lavine writes, "Every year I get countless tags on social media, texts, and frantic messages about people finding copperheads. Nine times out of ten the 'copperhead' is one of two harmless snakes; the DeKay's brown snake or the juvenile black racer snake and it ain't no copperhead. This misidentification happens frequently enough that as a team we decided to make this funny song about it."

The lyrics both admonish . . .

*You're standing there with that rake up in your hand? Tell me, sir, do you feel more like a man?*

and encourage . . .

*So put your shovels away cuz it's all good, they the best rat trap in the neighborhood!*

Stan Lake wrote the song. He's a North Carolina writer, filmmaker, photographer, and spiritual man who sees the divine in the wilderness and wants only to share that miracle with the world.

He said DeKay's brown snakes are secretive and small, coming out at night to eat snails and slugs. They're one of the most misidentified species, and copperhead is certainly a label they're often forced to wear. Stan said he receives requests to identify snakes all the time and that the sender will often argue with him when they're told it's not a venomous snake. He also said he's grown used to it.

"By and large, people see evil with snakes," he said. "And there's no changing that."

While Stan Lake doesn't know if his song will change attitudes, a few people have told him they've taken his message to heart and, as his lyrics plead, *let that little snakey grow.* He said saving even one snake makes his efforts worth it.

"Ain't No Copperhead" has yet to break the Billboard Hot 100, but I like to imagine it will, someday. Perhaps Catching Creation is coiled in the YouTube grass, biding their time, waiting for the right moment to strike the ears and hearts of anyone trotting around the garden with a post hole digger, a pair of loppers, and a desire for a damn good whacking.

It's silly to pretend the snakes aren't better at this wilderness thing than we are. They've had a few extra eons of practice when it comes to survival. At least, perhaps, we can let go of the notion that the only good snake is a dead snake and the only snake worth a breathless story is a "dangerous" one. Saw a brown snake in the herb garden? Hell yes! Rat snake in the garage? Damn right, buddy, get those mice. Northern water snake snoozing on the dock? Go get yourself a lotto ticket because it's your lucky day.

Live and let live, they say, but so far, the credo has yet to fully cover the creepy crawlies of the world—the sneakers, scuttlers, and slitherers. That includes copperheads and the snake you've mistaken for one. And while some might cite the seemingly grim statistic that the cucumber vipers account for about 40% of venomous snakebites in the US, only 0.1% of those are fatal. Often, the bites are dry, and most copperhead bites are the result of foot-to-body contact. You'd bitch if someone stepped on you, too, and as ecosystems succumb to human encroachment and development, wildlife encounters of all kinds increase. It helps to be alert. To pay attention to where we walk. Unfortunately, that's not our strong suit. We may talk a good game about wanting to move through the natural world with open eyes and silent steps, but even those of us who take pride in our nature awareness inevitably fail to see what's in front of us. This includes spiderwebs, copperheads, and that rusty, telescoping rake I stepped on in the high forests of Tucker County. (Nothing says "Wild and Wonderful" like a black eye and a tetanus shot.)

Perhaps I'm underestimating our appreciation for wild things. Perhaps these excitable reports aren't know-it-all bragging rights as much as they are the enthusiasm for a remarkable encounter. I'd *like* to believe that's why you're all dancing around the toolshed with your hoes held high. It's a celebration of life, of perfectly adapted, wonderfully camouflaged, beautifully built predators, right? All hail the copperheads, and their nonvenomous friends, too.

# Country Roads: A Brief Primer

R emember when John Denver strummed his guitar and the world fell in love with West Virginia, even if they couldn't find it on a map? The ubiquitous "Take Me Home, Country Roads" makes its way into every karaoke bar and Instagram post shared from a rural stretch of pavement. Thanks to Denver, a country road is both a romantic notion and a simple comfort. West Virginians love our country roads—and John Denver—more than anything. It's an official state song; it put West Virginia on the pop culture map. But no matter how romantic you think a winding, bucolic drive through the Mountain State might be, country roads here are no joke.

As you'll see, there's no easy way to get anywhere. Interstates touch the major cities, but to reach the good stuff, like ramp festivals and mystery holes and giant teapots, you'll travel on lesser roads, some of which will be paved and some of which will not. Certainly, none of them will be straight. And they're going to test you. So to prepare for this kind of travel, to drive on the country roads made famous in John Denver's beloved ballad, you're going to need a few things.

### *Fuel.*

There should be an option for cars in this state that changes the low-fuel warning light—which generally blinks on at twenty miles until empty, accompanied by a polite little *ding*—to something more attention-grabbing. Like an electric shock on the driver's buttocks. And a foghorn. And it needs to flash when you've got seventy miles until empty, because beyond the city limits, fueling opportunities fade. If you're on country roads and miss your opportunity to fill that tank, there's a decent chance you'll be well and truly screwed. Look at a cell coverage map of West Virginia—the kind of help you'll get will have to come from a passerby.

Despite the scarcity of rural gas stations, it's easy to push the limits. On a COVID-era vacation, we drove from Pendleton County to Greenbrier County. For us, this meant no souvenirs or groceries and only pay-at-the-pump gas stations. Easy enough. West Virginia's sparsely populated; we keep to ourselves.

On day four, we were down to one-third of a tank and, based on the planned 100-mile drive down the Allegheny Front, it was time to fuel. We pulled into a gas station with 120 miles left until empty, a level high enough to get us somewhere, but low enough to grab my attention, because while it reads 120 when you're coasting down a mountain, it drops to 63 when you're climbing up one. The numbers aren't reliable.

At the pump, however, there was a sign: Pay Inside. I crinkled my nose and fiddled with my mask. We'd been wearing them for months, but people inside might not be.

"Let's find a gas station where you just swipe your card," I said.

"Good call," the kids said.

It was a terrible call. But we headed south, confident we would find a gas station within the next thirty miles. That's a generous assumption in the mountains. Plus, we've got a phenomenon I call Gas Mirage. It happens when the fuel needle is hovering uncomfortably low on the dash. You're keeping your speed constant to maximize fuel efficiency and coasting down hills in neutral. The car has thirty-eight miles to empty, but there's a town ahead on the map where there must be fuel.

As you roll into town, you see the high roof of a gas station and its familiar hulking pumps. You rub the sweat from your brow—because things were getting pretty hairy—and thank the travel gods you've found salvation in this wild, green land where the roads wind and your phone searches endlessly for a signal it won't capture until the Virginia border. But the closer you come to the gas station, the emptier it and the entire town appear to be. Where is the hum of activity? Where are the people filling up, buying Moon Pies, and purchasing live bait? This glorious miracle that appeared in the nick of time sits motionless in the afternoon light. The garage is closed, the windows dusty and barren, and your relief flashes to horror as you realize this service station is abandoned, the disabled pumps empty of life-giving petrol. In fact, there's nothing in this town but seven cows and a rusting Sunoco, long bereft of fuel. You've been suckered in by the West Virginia Gas Mirage. Now, you've no choice but to continue to the next town, so distant on the map, and hope the gods will get you there. It'll be a terrifying leg of your journey. You'll fart

Deep & Wild

nervously into your seat, snap at the kids, and kill the air conditioner to save energy. If you're lucky, you'll find redemption before the tank runs dry.

As I searched for a gas station, the boys slept. I sat, rigid, observing the inversely proportional relationship between the number on the fuel gauge and the intensity of my anxious stomach cramps. I didn't know which would come first: the car hiccuping to a stop or my running off into the Monongahela National Forest to lighten the load on my digestive system from whichever end screamed loudest.

Sixty-seven minutes, three mountains coasted down in neutral, and two gas mirages later, with seventeen miles until empty, we spotted a gas station/mechanic/bait store/VFW/all-you-can-eat buffet/bakery/candle shop. I'd been on the verge of an emotional and intestinal breakdown. The pumps did not accept credit cards but, COVID be damned, we covered our faces and paid with cash—and gratitude—at the counter, used the restroom, and bought a strawberry-rhubarb pie.

### A paper map.

My dad taught me to use paper maps—a complement to my innate sense of direction. My husband, however, is directionally challenged. That's why he bought a Garmin, and God, I hate that thing. He named her Beulah, and that bitch loves to run roughshod over me. The stink of her smug superiority wafts all over the car.

Before we travel, I study a map and my trusty gazetteer and store them in the glove box—I'm a planner. Shawn lets Beulah do the thinking. He tells her where he wants to go, and she's happy to navigate. But occasionally, Beulah fucks up. Sometimes, construction alters the roads. Sometimes, her software needs an update. And sometimes, that travel trollop is just plain wrong, like the time she swore a decommissioned forest service road would get us over Laurel Mountain. Our Subaru ended up in a trench, nose-first, high on a ridge in Barbour County. After her abject failure, she seemed to know she'd screwed us and conveniently lost her signal for several hours.

That's another West Virginia quirk: GPS can lose signal. Notes on business websites often say, "Use our directions. Your GPS is wrong."

It happens. And even when they work, GPS units are not always trustworthy. In January of 2014, a fifty-eight-foot Dollar General delivery truck went astray in the mountains of Pocahontas County. The driver, a Mr. Jaime King of North Carolina, was hornswoggled by his own navigation system, which took him on the shortest route to his destination in the town of Marlinton. It did not, however, warn him about the narrowness, icy conditions, and hairpin turn his truck would skid off.

"This is my third time in West Virginia," King told the *Pocahontas Times*. "When it told me to take the back road, I said, 'Lord, Jesus. Lord, have mercy.'" Driver and truck were okay, thanks to his skill and levelheadedness, but with no cell service, he had to rely on the kindness of strangers, one of whom took him in for the night and fed him breakfast in the morning.

It's no wonder I don't trust Beulah. She's gotten us into similar trouble, and that hag has never once made me breakfast. What's more, I detect subtle attitude when we pick a route she has not endorsed.

"Recalculating," she grumbles. The way she says it reminds me of the way my mother used to sigh when she was mad at us. Instead of saying, "Hey, you deadbeats, get back here and do the dishes!" she simply exhaled a long gust of rage. And we knew we were in trouble. Likewise, Beulah gets fed up with us. She sounds like she's holding her nose when she says "recalculating." You can hear her disgust.

When it's me versus her, I go the way *my* internal compass directs, because I trust it. But when I'm wrong, it really sucks.

"Beulah says go right," Shawn will say.

"I disagree," I say back.

"Are you sure?" he asks.

"I just don't trust her." He's silent for a few moments as the paved road crumbles to gravel and the gravel dissolves into dirt.

"I think this is a game trail," Shawn says.

"It's not a game trail," I snap and keep driving. He bites his tongue for a few more minutes as rhododendrons scrape paint off the side of the car and the dirt softens into peat.

"Laura, we're in a bog."

"We're not in a bog. It's just a puddle."

"There's a beaver swimming past my window."

When water starts coming up through the floor, I'm forced to concede that I might have made a wrong turn somewhere. Shawn sits in the passenger seat, looking satisfied. He has unwavering faith in Beulah. He likes to have her on, in the background, because she orients him; I want to throw her in a creek. In the end, we compromised: she can stay on if he mutes her.

Recently, he bought a new Garmin. It speaks with a British accent and came with the name James. James doesn't have Beulah's attitude. He recalculates like a gentleman, with no audible irritation. I don't love him, but I'm pretty sure he'd hate that uppity Beulah if they met on the dashboard.

### Nerve.

West Virginia loves to build roads where roads should never be. We do a good job, but we seem to have trouble with the notion of two cars passing each other comfortably on the mountainside. I don't know if the original engineers simply miscalculated the width of a car—measure twice, cut once, fellas—but the wickedest roads are the ones with three components: dirt, a drop-off, and room for only one and a half vehicles. The problem is that most people drive a whole vehicle. And while downhill-facing drivers must yield by law, more likely, the person going up drives into the ditch and hopes they can climb out, while the person going down creeps toward the edge of the cliff in a white-knuckle, I-just-threw-up-in-the-footwell display of testicular fortitude.

One-lane roads are even worse. When you see another car coming, you both look for the nearest wide place. Etiquette dictates whoever is closest to the wide place pulls into it, and the car on the edge usually gets preference. Whenever we travel, I worry we'll encounter someone in an impossible, impassable space, where one of us must back up the mountain until we find some extra square footage. Backing up at length sucks to begin with, but when there's an axel-breaking ditch on one side and a sheer drop on the other, a fair amount of skill goes a long way toward keeping your tires on the ground.

Unfortunately, as with any sort of driving, the only way to gain skill is to practice, and the only way to practice not driving off a cliff is to drive *on* a cliff.

It's a flawed system.

***Faith.***

No matter how confident you are, your faith will eventually be tested on country roads. The deep forest, scarcity of other humans (or presence of sketchy ones), and lack of cell service will converge in your mind. You'll realize you made a mistake choosing this terrible, frightening road that leads only farther into God's country, except even God wouldn't come this far because there's nothing out here except cows and trees and dust. You'll wonder who the dumb idiot was that said, "Hey, let's see where this road goes." And then you'll realize that dumb idiot was you, but you were so much happier and so very naive, then, when you had signs and pavement and other cars around to remind you that you weren't alone in this wilderness.

But then you saw this road, and the mountain serpent offered you an apple that smelled like a shortcut through some pretty scenery, and you took it and ate it and now your eyes are open and you're in the middle of fucking nowhere and is this even a road any longer because it looks like a tractor path through a field and somebody feed my cat if I never make it back. Country roads are a test of faith, and you're going to lose it before the journey is over. And that's okay. You have to lose your faith in order to find it.

Even on my most exuberant days, when I know where I'm headed because I've plotted my route and checked it on two paper maps, a gazetteer, and Google, after 27 dusty miles, my faith falters. Doubt creeps in. On the map, the distance doesn't look too bad. But time, like the roads, bends and warps—it's physics. A country-road minute isn't 60 seconds—it's actually 413 seconds. So, when your parents promise, "10 more minutes," they're using West Virginia math and not the other kind of math that applies everywhere else in the universe.

A few years ago, we visited Spruce Knob. We noted a sign before the summit road: Spruce Knob, right, Spruce Knob Lake, left. We'd heard about Spruce Knob Lake: there's trout fishing, and it's popular with astral photographers because it's the darkest place in the eastern half of the US.

"It's only 8.5 miles down the road," I said. "GPS says 20 minutes. Let's check it out!"

On a good, packed-dirt road, you can go 25-30 miles per hour if the travel gods are with you. And for the first two miles, they were. Then, we hit a pothole.

Now, there are several distinct species of West Virginia pothole. The common species lives on paved roads in populated areas. Born in winter, it's about a foot in diameter. This is the pothole you hit unexpectedly, the one that ruins tires and breaks axles. It's the one you make passive-aggressive comments about to your husband, because even the kids could have spotted that crater, but he hit it dead-on in *your* car because he was pointing at a groundhog eating a daisy and not watching the road.

That's a hypothetical scenario, by the way. It in no way reflects an actual event that occurred near the town of Renick, West Virginia, at 4:17 p.m. on Sunday, July 5, 2020.

The potholes lurking on the road to Spruce Knob Lake that summer were a wilder species. Endemic to country roads and far larger than their pavement-born cousins, these holes are often wide and deep enough to serve as a practice run for the America's Cup trial should a sudden cloudburst strike. The holes' clustered nature—like pox, they gathered in groups for pothole solidarity—meant the posted 25 miles per hour was impossible. The speedometer dropped to 18, then 12, and finally, when the road took on the texture of an aged swiss cheese, 5 miles per hour. The car bounced unevenly. Ben hit his head on a fishing pole. Andy uttered a dramatic *ugh* every time the car lurched. Shawn grew increasingly irritated behind the wheel.

"This was a terrible idea," he growled. It was happening—he was losing faith, and the road was too narrow to turn around. This is why you need that paper map. You need to see, with your own eyes, that you'll find a town, eventually.

On a sidenote, it's important to remember this is a rural state. A town's name may be printed on the map in bold letters, but the intensity of the font is not indicative of its size or what might dwell there. The day Beulah led us into the trench in Barbour County, I pulled out my paper map and navigated us off the mountain. The roads were lonely and wild, but the map said we were headed toward a town called Pleasure Valley. I envisioned a mom-n-pop gas station, a diner with a faded sign advertising a plate of mashed potatoes and meatloaf for $3.99, and a quaint post office with red and blue trim staffed by a lovely woman named Helen.

In reality, the unincorporated community of Pleasure Valley, tucked into a hollow so tight you could barely see the sky, consisted of three cabins. And a fish farm.

We almost lost faith that day, just as we did on the way to Spruce Knob Lake. We said, "Shit, this is it, we're going to die out here." But we didn't. We made it. We were battered and cranky, and at least two of us had chewed on discarded french fries for sustenance, but we made it.

You must mentally and emotionally prepare for these journeys. There won't be cell service. You'll worry about your fuel level, your tires, your transmission, and your food supply. You might even pick a family member to eat first, should it come to that. (We did, and it's Andy.) But eventually, you'll find your way to that waterfall or fish farm. Remain faithful on country roads and gird yourself against despair. You'll get there.

I promise.

# Oh, Possum

In Harlan, Kentucky, artist Lacy Hale designed a city mural depicting a flowing green pokeweed and a baby opossum. Ripening berries dot the plant's purple stem and the opossum hangs by its feet, reaching for the fruit. She chose pokeweed, a local species, in honor of the town's annual Poke Sallet Festival; she chose an opossum because she thought they were cool animals and installed the mural on an aging brick wall in 2019.

The community complained. Loudly. About the opossum. They bemoaned the implied association with a roadkill-prone, rodent-like, garbage thief. A local Appalachian studies professor said his students had "a lot of feelings" about the image.

Opossums tend to do that. Perhaps it's because, for all our modern conveniences and technology, we still identify with animals. Each state has an official bird, an official mammal, an official fish. We feel warmly about them and imagine we share their best qualities. It's true on a regional scale, too: bison symbolize the American West, moose represent the northern woods, and the South claims the alligator, among others. But Appalachia doesn't have an animal. There's been no creature set aside for the old mountains and hollows, for scrappy mountaineers to claim as our own.

I propose the opossum. Focused, adaptable, and persistent, the opossum makes a fitting Appalachian symbol, though they may not get much support as candidates. Much like Ben Franklin's unsuccessful attempt to make the turkey our national bird, opossums don't have that distinguished look you want in a representative species. They lack the bulk and power of the black bear, the mystery of the bobcat, and the jewel tones of the wily brook trout. Indeed, opossums are odd, a creature an exhausted God might have thrown together with parts leftover from a busy week of creation. Whatever He had lying around the shop (grippy hands, snaky tail, crippling anxiety), He chucked into the opossum and sent it down to the Garden of Eden to tip over Adam's garbage cans and eat the cat food off Eve's back porch. It's an animal so weird, so remarkable, and so frequently maligned that it has earned a notable place in our culture simply by being itself.

Sound familiar, West Virginia? Kentucky?

The Virginia opossum is the only marsupial endemic to the US and Canada. The fossil record indicates that the ancestors of all marsupials began to appear and evolve in what would become North America around the time of the dinosaurs' extinction. It's a lot of history for a little garbage eater.

They live solitary lives, coming together only to breed. Joeys are born almost neonatal and must make their way to their mother's pouch to finish their gestation. After two and a half months, they emerge, all ears and eyes and fur. For the rest of their short childhoods, their mother cares for them and teaches them how to be proper opossums. And how does a dedicated mom shuttle up to twenty long-tailed toddlers around in a busy world? On her back. She meanders along, like an overcrowded bus riding low on its frame, and will have up to three annual litters over the course of her brief lifespan, which may be only a year or two.

Opossums are almost universally immune to rabies, impervious to snake venom, and they eat up to five thousand ticks per year, making them vital to curbing the spread of Lyme disease. As scavengers, they do their part to keep things tidy; they'll eat most anything, including but not limited to vegetation, fish, carrion, insects, and rodents. It's why they're drawn to humans and our lazy leavings—they're opportunists and we're slobs. Perhaps because they're a Miocene epoch throwback—a living fossil that has changed little over the eons—they seem foreign and weird. It's no wonder they fascinated early European settlers.

Captain John Smith, founder of the colony of Jamestown in 1607, wrote to England about the bizarre creatures populating the New World. "An Opassom hath an head like a Swine, and a taile like a Rat, and is of the bignes of a Cat," he told the folks back home. During his tenure as president, George Washington attempted several times to send a pair of opossums to a friend in Ireland, but it's unlikely they survived the journey. Thomas Jefferson requested opossums be sent to France as gifts when he served as minister and admitted to tormenting them as a child. President Benjamin Harrison is said to have owned two opossums named Mr. Reciprocity and Mr. Protection, though evidence points to their presence for culinary purposes rather than cuddle buddies.

Theodore Roosevelt went with a different mammal. His emblem, the "Teddy" bear, came about when he refused to shoot a bear tied to a tree. By the time William Howard Taft succeeded him, teddy bears were as popular as TR himself.

Billy Possum was Taft's answer to his predecessor's beloved bear. At an Atlanta presidential banquet at which guests were served an opossum dinner (the president was said to have inhaled his and later reported smooth digestion of the cooked critter), Taft was presented with a stuffed opossum (the kind filled with cotton, not breading) to kick off his Teddy Bears Suck campaign, designed to discredit Roosevelt and his signature snuggly toy. Taft went low—presidential propaganda postcards depicted Billy Possum eating poor Teddy. TR had the last laugh, though, because *his* furry creature had earned him a gentle, merciful reputation, while Taft's possum served only to remind constituents that he could eat one in under six minutes.

More recently, President Herbert Hoover kept an opossum among his White House pets. Per the Herbert Hoover Presidential Library and Museum, Billy Possum (yes, a second one) was a wild opossum minding his own business when he stumbled onto the White House lawn. The Hoovers adopted him, and he spent his days in a pen that former President Coolidge had built for his pet raccoon, Rebecca. In a generous display of sportsmanship, Hoover loaned Billy to a Maryland high school whose own marsupial mascot had disappeared. Without their lucky opossum, the school's various athletic teams endured a string of devastating losses, the course of which was reversed when Billy arrived from Washington.

Clearly, Americans in bygone eras kept opossums as both pets and meals. In our modern vehicular times, however, we're far more likely to encounter a flat one on the road. Flatties come in the millions: one study indicated that between four and eight million opossums meet their destiny on the highways of America each year. They've got poor vision, travel at night, and scavenge in the street, so it's bound to end badly.

Every spring, hopeful "pouch pickers" take to the roads. These intrepid souls pull over when they see a victim and check for babies, which can live for several days after their mother has died. Rehabilitators care for them and return the survivors to the wild when they're old enough. This is usually how people come to have an opossum in their home. A biologist friend rescued one, and just as I was about to invite myself over, the opossum showed herself the door. Or, rather, the window.

I volunteered as a zoo docent in the early nineties, and the opossums were my favorite animal to showcase. Often, they drew negative reactions, so we had been trained to deflect criticism with education. We recited a host of opossum facts whenever visitors—usually middle-class moms with designer sandals and acrylic nails—squealed in disgust. It was the same complaint, over and over: they're ugly and they have rat tails.

The opossum's prehensile tail is an evolutionary wonder. They use it for counterbalance, as a fifth limb when climbing, and to carry or grasp things like food, a limb, or a tree trunk. (Their opposable hallux—a clawless toe not unlike a thumb—aids in climbing as well.) Opossums can indeed hang by their tails, but only for short periods. It's not strong enough to hold them while they sleep, nor do they sleep upside down. Also, it's not naked; it's covered in fine hairs.

The Northern Cherokee Nation's origin story recalls that the opossum's tail was once covered in soft, lustrous fur. The other animals invited him to a council meeting, and he agreed to go only if he would be given a special seat so everyone could admire it. In secret, the other animals sent the cricket to cut all the tail's hair off. When the opossum arrived at the council and began to brag, the other animals laughed. He turned to see his naked tail and was too embarrassed to speak, so he lay down and pretended to be dead.

I suppose it's a lesson for all of us: be humble, because vanity is not a good look. Neither is lying on the ground in a dramatic puddle of drool.

No matter the opossum's origin, they're always among us. Their nocturnal habits mean our paths rarely cross, but it's not uncommon to find one trapped in a garbage can or lurking under the porch. The opossum is a timid varmint; when confronted, it opens its mouth in a hiss and reveals a jaw full of sharp teeth. But that's about it. The display is nothing more than a bluff—they rarely bite. It may then move on to

Deep & Wild

drooling to convince the predator that it's sick. The next line of defense is to lie down and die and emit an odor of decay; "playing possum" is their signature move, and it must work, because the comical ability to feign death has kept them going for sixty-five million years.

Nevertheless, opossum prejudice lingers. They've been maligned since someone came up with the idea of weekly garbage collection. They're master scavengers, which is why they fit right into human society—no animal worth its fleas would pass up a readily available source of stinky sustenance served in a giant silver dish every Monday night at 10 p.m. And while you'll find them in your garbage cans, you'll also find them on your porch with a mouth full of pet food. A friend found one in her kitchen. The intruder came through the pet door, and she posted a Facebook picture of it atop one of her kitchen shelves. It looks concerned.

Opossums seem to worry a lot. Whereas a raccoon struts around and will snarl and bark when threatened—then saunter off in a huff—the opossum seems embarrassed to be discovered. Like a celebrity caught coming out of a plastic surgeon's office, the opossum turns away, mortified, in nervous defeat—*Oh dear, what do I do now? This is awful.*

I met one such marsupial on my back porch, at dawn. I called him Eugene, and while there was no easy way to know if he was male or female (I might have felt around for a bifurcated uterus, but that seemed a little forward since we'd never been formally introduced), his "bignes" indicated male. I had just let the dogs out and taken a moment to breathe in the morning stillness. When I turned back toward the door, I came face to face with Eugene, perched on the railing. We stared at each other for a millisecond, as humans and animals do when they take each other by surprise.

Annie Dillard had an encounter like this with a weasel, recounted in her essay, "Living Like Weasels."

> Our look was as if two lovers, or deadly enemies, met unexpectedly on an overgrown path when each had been thinking of something else: a clearing blow to the gut. It was also a bright blow to the brain, or a sudden beating of brains, with all the charge and intimate grate of rubbed balloons. It emptied our lungs. It felled the forest, moved the fields, and drained the pond; the world dismantled and tumbled into that black hole of eyes.

Annie Dillard is an incredible writer. She looks fabulous in a hat, and I have no doubt she can fold a perfect fitted sheet. But I don't buy it, because I saw a weasel on a dusty Ohio road, and our look was not one of lovers or enemies. It was more like, *Look at that funky squirrel!* and *Holy shit, she's going to run me down!*

Likewise, I imagine Eugene's mental state in those quick moments before I noticed him. *Oh no. This is bad. This is really bad.* With no other recourse, he hurled himself off the second-story porch. For a millisecond, his gray fur rippled in the morning breeze. Then, *splat.* I hurried to the rail, expecting to see his broken body lying in my northern sea oats. But he righted himself, scurried to the edge of the deck, and squeezed under it.

I'm an introvert, so I can relate. Lately, they've been popping up in memes about anxiety and social aversion; I don't know if social media algorithms are merely delivering what I desire or if the internet has finally discovered the opossum's cringey relatability. But they're catching on. Build-A-Bear Workshop announced in 2021 a new critter, the "awesome opossum." And the more opossums I see, the more I hope one will wander into my life. It's illegal in most states to keep one without a wildlife rehabilitator's license, and opossum care can be tricky. They're solitary creatures who need their own space, and they do best out there, in the wild. Nevertheless, the opossum thrives among humans because it's so adaptable. It eats most anything, reproduces frequently, sleeps wherever, swims, climbs, crawls, and moseys. And whether we like the comparison or not, the opossum reflects our own Appalachian nature to survive by doing whatever it has to.

Wildlife biologist Durward L. Allen once called the opossum "a sluggish, smelly, disreputable critter without a semblance of character or self-respect." (If basic manners reflect character, then Dr. Allen was no prize petunia, either.) But opossums score higher than dogs on tests of memory and ability to find food. Yet only recently have amazing opossum facts made it past the pages of a scientific study. Their fans are growing in number, and we Appalachians are missing out. A creature that has flourished despite the arrival of man and the complete unwilding of their ecosystem parallels the obstinate tenacity of mountain people, who stare down hardship and adversity. Yet Appalachians are just as likely as anyone to revile the opossum. When Knott County, Kentucky, named the opossum its official animal in the 1980s, people lamented its low intelligence as a poor reflection on the state. Anchoring such an animal to a frustrated region desperate for respect was no better than seeing Jed and Granny Clampett boil one up in their Beverly Hills mansion for primetime television laughs.

Or displaying one on a brick wall downtown.

Opossums don't waste their brief days on irony, though. They've seen epochs turn and continents rise and fall. Once, they scurried away from sharp-toothed carnivores and towering terror birds. Now, they weave their way through our neighborhoods and across our highways, living short, quiet lives. The risks and rewards, pickings and predators, have changed. But still, the opossum persists.

# The West Virginia Brown Dog

Rescue dogs in West Virginia come in all shapes, sizes, and breed configurations, but there's one thing you'll notice when you survey your choices: most of them are brown. More specifically, their hues roll along the color wheel, from ecru to tan to the color of wet dirt, but basically, what you've got is a mess of brown dogs to choose from.

I have one of these brown dogs. She's dog number three. Does anybody really need three dogs? Probably not. Two is manageable, and we had two. Then, I got that assignment.

Admittedly, it was my idea to write about a local rescue called the Road Home Animal Project for a northern West Virginia publication. I asked the rescue president to bring a foster dog to our interview for a photo. She brought Minnie. Minnie wore a green tartan puffer coat. Her ears stuck out from the sides of her head, like Yoda's, and her dark eyes sat large on her face. She trotted along with us at the park as we talked, sniffing the ground and winding her leash around our legs. She'd been in foster care for several months, and her siblings had been adopted. The rescue couldn't understand why nobody wanted her.

By the end of our interview, someone did.

Minnie's arrival unleashed chaos. Within weeks, our house was trashed, our carpets stained. My wooden spoons were splintered, and the remote control looked like it had been gnawed by an angry beaver. Sleeping in on Saturday mornings was out of the question, as was sleeping alone. (I'd assumed Minnie would sleep in her crate, but when I went back and read the "Where Puppy Will Sleep" clause in my puppy contract, it clearly said, "Puppy will sleep on human's pillow, without exception.")

*What have I done?* I asked myself. *Life was so simple. Everybody was house-trained and nobody chased the cats and all the kids' stuffed animals had heads.* I yearned for my old, easy life as I shivered in the snow at two o'clock in the morning while she sniffed the ground, too distracted to pee. I mourned as I fired up the carpet steamer—again—and chased her through the supermarket parking lot when she leapt out of the car. I wondered why I thought I needed a puppy. Not that she kept her puppy body long—within months she'd gone from twiggy to barrel-shaped, and her head began to catch up with her ears, growing into a dense cube she used to whack our knees and butt the cats away from their bowls. She was appealing in a funny-looking way, but it was hard to figure out what Minnie was. On the inside.

Technically, Minnie's a mixed breed, but here in the Mountain State, she's what's known as a West Virginia Brown Dog. The West Virginia Brown Dog may not be recognized by the American Kennel Club, but it's a real thing. So real, in fact, that the Kanawha-Charleston Humane Association declared June 20, 2013, "West Virginia Brown Dog Day," in honor of our state's one hundred fiftieth birthday. Shelter visitors could adopt a West Virginia Brown Dog for twenty dollars. The ads didn't include a formal description of the discounted canines, but they didn't need to. West Virginians know one when we see it.

The West Virginia Brown Dog is smallish but sometimes biggish. It's sturdy but possibly delicate or, conversely, a brutish lug. It's not petite—unless it is—and it's usually somewhere between Labrador- and chihuahua-sized. It probably has hound in its DNA, which you'll see in the way it follows its nose, and pit bull, which you'll see in the shape of its skull. The West Virginia Brown Dog is adaptable, loyal, ornery. It's a well-tempered, squirrel-chasing counter-surfer. It rides in trucks and Subarus and canoes. It hikes, goes to the office, and sleeps on your furniture. You can dress it in a sweater, sports jersey, or puffer jacket; West Virginia Brown Dogs go with everything.

The rescue advertised Minnie as a miniature pinscher mix, and as she grew into weird proportions, we imagined what other breeds might lurk in her DNA. I saw beagle. We all saw American pit bull terrier in her stoutness and clownish behavior. But the West Virginia Brown Dog recipe can have many ingredients, and puppies often come from a long line of other West Virginia Brown Dogs, so it can be difficult to identify which purebred ancestor claims responsibility for a block head or curly tail. Overcome by curiosity, we ordered a doggy DNA test, swabbed her cheek, and waited.

I think we're fond of these brown dogs because we see ourselves in them. Not only in their scrappy, adaptable nature, but also because the ancestry of a West Virginia Brown Dog reads a lot like that of a

Deep & Wild

multigeneration West Virginian. Swab our cheeks and you'll find a heavy dose of Scots-Irish heritage, a good bit of German and English, and a smattering of Welsh, Swiss, Polish, Italian, Hungarian, and African American. You'll also hear a variety of accents. In my hometown of Wheeling, many speak as Pittsburghers do: my grandfather, a Harvard-educated, fourth-generation Wheeling native, *worshed* his clothes and trimmed the *booshes*. In the central and southern parts of the state, you'll hear the speech of Appalachia, traditionally referred to as Appalachian English. Some scholars have claimed it's an archaic Elizabethan throwback. In 1978, Dr. Cratis D. Williams of Appalachian State University wrote, "the dialect of the Appalachian people is the oldest living English dialect, older than the speech of Shakespeare, closer to the speech of Chaucer." That's debatable. More likely, the dialect evolved from the speech of those Scots-Irish ancestors, and variations exist within the different regions of Appalachia. North Carolinians sound noticeably different from West Virginians because, like West Virginia Brown Dogs, little about Appalachian English is uniform, not even the way Appalachians pronounce the word "Appalachia."

Most Appalachians say *Appa-latch-uh*, and many feel that if you say it with a short *a*, you're a true Appalachian; if you say it with a long *a*—as in, *Appa-lay-shuh*—you're an outsider. Sharyn McCrumb, an Appalachian author from North Carolina, went as far as to say, "*Appa-lay-shuh* is the pronunciation of condescension, the pronunciation of the imperialists, the people who do not want to be associated with the place, and the pronunciation *Appa-latch-uh* means that you are on the side that we trust." Not everyone agrees.

*Appalachia North* author Matthew Ferrence grew up in western Pennsylvania. One might not immediately think of Pennsylvania, northern West Virginia, eastern Ohio, western Maryland, and southern New York as Appalachia, but, per the Appalachian Regional Commission (ARC), they are. In Ferrence's memoir, he recalls grad school at West Virginia University, where he learned from other Appalachians that he'd been pronouncing the word incorrectly. The realization reframed what he thought he knew about himself and his fellow Pennsylvanians.

". . . I grew up among Appalachians who pronounced ourselves as *App-uh-lay-shuns*. What does it mean when you grew up as a boy saying the word *wrong*? What does it mean when you're from a place where everyone did?" Ferrence considers the notion that he and his fellow northern Appalachians were, therefore, "bad Appalachians, deniers of our heritage, willful self-exiles." But Appalachian scholars, he writes, agree that there's no correct pronunciation, despite what the McCrumb crowd crows.

The debate isn't likely to be resolved, even in West Virginia. Like its signature brown dog, the state may be more easily defined by what it *isn't* than what it is. And it's not just the state's inhabitants and their linguistics that are a mixed breed—it's West Virginia itself. Because nobody is quite sure where we fit in this country, geographically speaking. Not even us.

West Virginia is the only state that lies entirely within Appalachia (as defined by the ARC). On a long day trip, you could travel through South Central Appalachia, Central Appalachia, North Central Appalachia, and arrive in my neck of the woods in northern Appalachia, having never left the state. Four of the five ARC-defined regions cover West Virginia territory, making us an Appalachian Brown Dog, too.

In terms of region, the US Census Bureau lists West Virginia as a Southern Atlantic state. However, the "West" in West Virginia came about because we chose to *leave* the South. Still, southern West Virginians may identify with the South anyway, while northern West Virginians feel like northerners. Americans from more extreme latitudes would probably disagree; culturally, West Virginia couldn't be more different from New York or New England. So, when asked, we offer a vague quip about being the northernmost of the southern states and the southernmost of the northern states and leave it at that.

In terms of latitude, we're too mountainous, our land too crinkled by plate tectonics and erosion, to be considered central, like our immediate neighbors in Ohio. Some—like the Bureau of Labor Statistics—call us a mid-Atlantic state, but the foreboding Allegheny Front shields us from the busyness and density of the other mid-Atlantic states, and we remain a quiet vacation spot for DC residents. The Federal Trade Commission labels us "east central," with Ohio and Michigan. The US Office of Management and Budget lumps eastern West Virginia counties in with cities like Cumberland, Maryland; Alexandria and Arlington,

Virginia; and Washington, DC, itself, for statistical purposes. How could we possibly know where we belong? The only thing we truly know is that none of these out-of-state places feel much like West Virginia.

Regardless, something changes when we leave West Virginia. Regional differences within the state cease to divide us. Our home is the common thread in our mixed-breed DNA, the reason why, when expats and college kids return, they inevitably take a photo of the "Wild, Wonderful" sign at the state line and post it with a hashtag like #CountryRoadsTakeMeHome. Beyond our borders, we're all just West Virginians, defined by our inability to fit anywhere else.

West Virginia is the mutt. The proud brown dog that declared independence in 1863 and continues to do so. Don't call us western Virginia. We aren't Pittsburgh or DC. We're West-by-God Virginia, locked in by rivers and mountains, curving and windy and infuriatingly impassable without a map and Dramamine. We like our hot dogs with mustard and slaw and our actual dogs vague and mud-colored. Like Minnie.

The results of Minnie's DNA test surprised us. I was wrong—she isn't beagle. She *is* golden retriever and miniature pinscher and pit bull. The other ingredients include chihuahua, American Eskimo dog, boxer, pug, and something the lab calls a supermutt, which may be American bulldog and/or Cesky terrier. There's a lot of room for uncertainty, and we never know which breed is causing the behaviors we laugh at. Certainly, Minnie wouldn't be what she is without those breeds, but even if we could define her, each West Virginia Brown Dog is more than the sum of its twisting chromosomes.

When I started including #WVBrownDog in social media postings, I discovered other West Virginia Brown Dog owners whose loving companions look like mine. They're out there. And while some states have chosen an official breed, as North Carolina did with the Plott hound, the West Virginia senate adopted a resolution in 2020 to designate an official state canine: the humble shelter dog. They are brown. They are motley—mutts born to mutts born to mutts. The breed standard, if one existed, would list but one essential characteristic: a loyal heart bred in West Virginia.

# Poor, Illiterate, and Strung Out

I got the tattoo the same week Bette Midler started talking shit about West Virginia. Furious at Democratic Senator Joe Manchin's 2021 refusal to support President Biden's Build Back Better plan, she tweeted her fury, likely from her penthouse in the Upper East Side.

"What #JoeManchin, who represents a population smaller than Brooklyn, has done to the rest of America, who wants to move forward, not backward, like his state, is horrible. He sold us out. He wants us all to be just like his state, West Virginia. Poor, illiterate and strung out," she wrote.

I'm almost pathologically nonconfrontational, but I got on Twitter at 1 a.m. in my bed and told Bette Midler—whose talents I've always adored—to go to hell. Then I posted her tweet on Facebook. Within minutes, a few of my fellow West Virginians replied. Some were incensed. Others pushed back.

"She's absolutely right."

"The people of West Virginia keep voting for the leaders that keep them oppressed."

"We have no one to blame but ourselves."

I thought about replying, but I didn't want to wake up the next morning to a long, sour debate, so I deleted the post. I wondered if Senator Manchin had read Bette Midler's tweet from his bed in his sixty-five-foot yacht, called *Almost Heaven*.

My kids were shocked when I came home with a tattoo on my side at age forty-two. It was my first, and though I'd expected pain during the process, I was surprised by the way it lingered. The new wound felt sunburned. Scorched. My skin snarled with rage at this, the latest in a series of physical blunders. *First, the hot pan, then the slipped kitchen knife, now a bazillion, painted puncture wounds. Why do you do this to yourself?*

I wondered if I would keep this new art private. My family doesn't love tattoos, and this isn't uncommon. Despite the rising popularity of body art—almost 50 percent of millennials and 30 percent of Americans have tattoos—the negative attitude toward the inked persists. Multiple studies have looked at modern sentiments about tattoos. When presented with images of tattooed people, subjects in the study perceived them as heavy drinkers, promiscuous, and found them less attractive than images of the same people with their tattoos digitally erased. Notably, even subjects with tattoos of their own viewed other tattooed individuals negatively. Other studies have revealed that tattooed women are judged more harshly than tattooed men; they're perceived as less intelligent, less honest, and less caring.

When I was in college in the late nineties, many of my female classmates got lower back tattoos—the kind pejoratively referred to as tramp stamps. I bought one for a friend on her birthday, but that was the closest I came to getting one of my own. I couldn't think of anything I wanted to put on my body that would be there when I was sixty-five, when I was eighty. It'd be there on my cold corpse in the funeral home, faded and mushy.

I once heard an ink-loving woman say, "When people warn me not to get a tattoo because it'll look terrible when I'm old, I say, 'Everything on our bodies will look terrible when we're old!'" I admired the sentiment, but I still liked my skin unmarked.

Then one day, that changed. I found something I *did* want to put on my body forever. I was ready. I chose my artist—a talented woman in a local shop—consulted with her about the design, and booked the appointment, which took several hours.

When the tattoo was finished, I sat up. Middle-aged hip sockets and knee joints howled with stiffness as I waddled over to the full-length mirror, pants around my thighs. With a deep breath, I looked down at the image I would wear for the rest of my life.

🌿

West Virginia's topography ranges from hilly plateau to imposing mountains, but its highest elevations lie along the Allegheny Front, in the east. Here the earth is wrinkled in a series of long ridges and valleys that run for twelve-hundred miles. The region stopped settlers in their tracks, limiting their westward progress to rare passes like the Cumberland Gap, far to West Virginia's south.

The Allegheny Front is a ferocious, blustery place, where red spruce crown the highest knobs. These dark green conifers grow to 130 feet and thrive in cold temperatures. Red spruce once covered all of West Virginia's high places—one million acres of them—but 95% of the original forests were logged, and climate change threatens the remaining patches, as do invasive insects and acid rain.

Spruce smell indescribably wild—cold and peaty and sweet. They smell like rocks. They smell like moss. And those that grow on the Allegheny Front are forever altered by the harsh conditions. The winds scream through the forests with such intensity that the spruce are flagged; their branches only grow on the trees' eastern side. These trees have survived a century of decimation and learned to flourish in adversity. To be born on the Allegheny Front is a privilege and a burden; the wildest, most beautiful creatures pay a heavy price to exist there, surrendering a part of themselves to the forces of nature. But what does grow is full and strong and will sustain them for their 450-year lifespan. The red spruce's reality is one of hardship, of standing in the blasting face of extreme conditions and thriving by adaptation, whatever that adaptation looks like.

This was the image I etched into my body—three flagged red spruce perched atop a West Virginia peak, standing against the wind, framed by a flaming sunrise.

If Bette Midler anticipated backlash from her tweet, her expectations couldn't have matched the roar that arose from West Virginians. Conservatives responded. Liberals responded. The tourist industry. Businesses. Entrepreneurs. Academics. They took to Twitter and posted photos of the New River Gorge. Of mountains and streams. Of a meme depicting a knuckled fist, extended middle finger, and jutting left thumb, a defiant gesture that reproduces the state's unique shape. And they quickly dug up stats that revealed West Virginia's literacy rates are notably higher than those in several other states, including Texas and California.

Despite the divisiveness of the times and the political leanings of the Mountain State, the unification happened in an instant. For most West Virginians, partisanship had little to do with the response. We recoiled, collectively, like the timber rattlesnakes hiding in our high country. We rattled. We hissed. And, as always, we defended ourselves. We knew it probably wouldn't change any minds, but we invited Bette and the league of detractors to come to West Virginia and see where their arrows had landed.

Midler quickly apologized to the "good people of West Virginia" for her outburst. She said she was seeing red, that Joe Manchin was a criminal, and that we deserved better. Lots of people agreed that Joe Manchin was a criminal, while others defended him, but I didn't believe Bette Midler genuinely thought we deserved better—she'd hurled too big a stone. And while some accepted her apology, the damage was done. We licked our wounds and posted TikToks about why we love this place. And we didn't check each other's voter registration cards before we liked a photo or commented our support of one another. We rallied, a small but scrappy clan of mountaineers used to scorn, derision, and struggle.

To that end, nothing about being West Virginian is easy. When settlers arrived, they found steep mountains, heavily forested, and the gentler land beyond guarded by the imposing Allegheny Front. Miners dug their paychecks out of the belly of the earth, paying the highest price for accidents and missteps. The harder they worked, the tighter the fists of the coal companies squeezed. People have been literally carving out a living for centuries here. And while they were carving, cutting, digging, and scraping, someone else was reaping the rewards, assuring them that America's lights were on because of their hard work and sacrifice. Promising them they didn't need anything beyond the coal companies to keep them afloat. The country desperately needed West Virginia's vital black rock, so we shipped it out—except for the chunks the poorest families scavenged from the side of the railroad tracks and coal tipples. In time, coal companies began to slice off the tops of mountains to reach the coal—overburden, they call the green earth above the seam— and leave behind a poisoned, empty moonscape. Now, the oil and gas companies tell the same story as they pipeline their way through backyards and forests. The industry still takes whatever it can and sends it away, while West Virginia keeps nothing but empty promises, toxic slag heaps, and medical bills.

We figured Bette Midler didn't know much about that.

Over the next two weeks, I took meticulous care of the tattoo, cleaning it, moisturizing it, and protecting it. I eschewed underwear for twelve days so nothing would rub against it and interfere with the healing process, which was far more extensive than I'd anticipated. It itched without mercy, and Reddit suggested I slap the injured skin in lieu of scratching. After a few days, the tattoo crusted over and began to peel in black and green and orange flakes. Scabs grew in the spots that had seen the most abuse, the places of trauma where the shading needles scraped the skin over and over again, leaving it raw and seeping with a foreign pigment. It went from stunning to looking like crap, but my artist assured me that my body would heal, and the final product would be striking.

On day eleven, I had to put on underwear and real pants. Within minutes, a seam rubbed against one of the largest scabs and tore it off. Blood oozed out and ran down my leg. I panicked. Tattoo artists remind their clients to let the scabs fall off on their own and never to pick at them. Removing a scab prematurely not only leaves the wound open to infection and slows the healing process, but it can also pull the ink out of the skin. The result is a blurred or bare spot in an otherwise beautiful piece of art. Ultimately, it's an easy fix the artist can touch up once the tattoo has healed—it's not the end of the world. But this was my first tattoo, and I'd done the very thing I wasn't supposed to do. I'd damaged my beautiful red spruce trees, pulled the color from the sky above their flagged branches.

"It's okay," the tattoo shop assistant assured me. "Put some gauze on it and protect it from abrasion. We can touch it up for you when it's healed. Just take care of it as best you can and see what happens." I was furious with myself. I should have protected this thing that had become so important to me. I pictured a healed tattoo scarred by lumpy, pitted skin. It wouldn't matter how lovely and delicate the rest of the work was—eyes would be drawn to the ugly parts.

It wouldn't be the only messed up tattoo out there. Bad tattoos abound, and there are plenty of bad tattoo websites. Clickbait may attract us to them, but schadenfreude keeps us on the page. We've been enjoying the minor misfortunes of others since *America's Funniest Home Videos* premiered thirty years ago, and not much has changed.

The best bad tattoos are always the ones spelled incorrectly. *No Regerts. Live You're Life.* Characters in Mandarin that are supposed to mean *courage* but actually mean *cheese danish.* They're called "hilariously bad tattoos," and we can't help but wonder if the tattooee even realizes what they've done. Or what's been done *to them*, because when a tattoo turns out poorly, when it's misspelled or ugly or tacky, the human canvas—not the artist—owns the mistake for life. Even if the client gave the artist proper spelling or a clear photo to replicate, the person wearing the bad tattoo gets the blame.

"Why did you get it?"

"Do you even realize it's misspelled?"

"*Can* you spell?"

We usually assume the tattooee isn't aware of the glaring mistake on their forearm or that they're genuinely happy with the mangled portrait that makes their dearly departed sister's face look like Freddie Krueger in an infrared sauna. More importantly, when we scroll through these hilariously bad tattoos, it's all too easy to abandon our empathy and conclude that these people probably deserve what they've gotten.

Bette Midler once tweeted, "Is it true that tattoos have to be re-touched every few years? Ouch! Ah me, after forty, it's patch, patch, patch . . ."

Improving oneself comes at a price. I paid $200 for the red spruce tattoo. A coal miner with black lung receives $737 per month in compensation. (Coincidentally, that's just enough to cover a round of Botox, should they express an interest in fixing up their roughest parts.) A tweet is 280 characters long, and that's more than enough space to stereotype. To wound. It's not nearly enough, however, to mount a defense. You can't explain poverty in 280 characters. Desperation. The dark choice between heat and food and insulin—only one, not two, impossible to get all three. The resigned certainty of black lung tomorrow so you can feed your kids today. Most of all, a tweet can't explain how 160 years of unfortunate history has led to an inescapable present, and that life here doesn't simply boil down to a poor choice made by an ignorant people who deserve what we've gotten.

Vote blue, we heard. It's the only way things will change. We voted blue, we voted Manchin into office instead of the red guy. Still, we hear the same criticisms.

*West Virginians will never escape their wretchedness until they start making better choices.*

The illusion is that we've had choices.

As predicted, my body finished the first stage of healing. The scabs fell off, the rough edges softened, and there was no visible damage from the underwear incident. I could finally run my hand along the curve of my hip and feel smooth, fresh skin. The crimson sunrise behind the spruce trees, the lichen on the rocks, lit with dawn's glow, the deep, dark green of the branches . . . every glimpse of it filled me with purpose. I'd finally done it. I'd committed to West Virginia, and now, wherever I went, would carry it with me.

The illusion was that I could have left it behind. We don't leave this place—not fully. We wear the mark of our home, and whether that image is perfectly crafted or marred by a glaring error, it's there. For life. And West Virginia's lot is not Bette Midler's fault. She's only rage tweeting, from afar. Today, it's her pointing finger; tomorrow, it'll be someone else's. Some days, we even tweet at one another from within and wonder, in 280 characters, why we all choose to live here, to wear such a mark of shame.

My skin will take six more months to fully heal from the trauma of approximately 720,000 tiny cuts, and even then, I'll need to shield my tattoo from the sun's intensity. And while I'll always bear the image of my home, I'm fortunate—I can choose to reveal it or keep it to myself. It can stay a beautiful secret. I don't need to unpack what this place means. I don't need to explain what we know so well: wild creatures here stand against the fiercest wind and grow in spite of it.

# Pure, Unadulterated Garbage

When I was getting my MFA, I read a ton of place-based writing, and nowhere in American literature features more prominently than the western desert. There's just something about the desert—its hugeness, its fullness, its emptiness. The color, the starkness, the red slickrock.

Western writers also love the coyote and its ancient lore. Coyote Man is woven into the narratives of the indigenous peoples of the West. He's a wise man, he's a trickster, he's a randy old bugger. And as I read my way through myriad lyrical, desert meditations in my graduate writing program, he popped up on every page, so wrapped in metaphor and symbolism that I couldn't tell where the legend ended and the writer's love affair began.

Honestly, I'm a little tired of Coyote. You know he never caught that road runner, right? Maybe I'm too much of an easterner to get it. Maybe I'm a little salty about Coyote Man because, here in West Virginia, we don't have his equivalent. We do have coyotes, but they're not slight, wily creatures that bound over the slickrock. Ours are more likely to bound into the backyard and abscond with an urban chicken.

The coyote's journey to West Virginia began when the western coyote moved eastward, up through Canada, and then down into Appalachia. The timber wolves that once inhabited the region were extirpated in the 1800s, when the American frontier mentality was all about killing predators rather than understanding their role in the ecosystem. Wolves and mountain lions were shot by the thousands, which left an opening for another large carnivore. When the western coyote arrived, it bred with the remaining red wolves in the south, timber wolves in the north, and dogs. The result was a new cover of an old song: the eastern coyote.

When it comes to genetics, Dr. Roland Kays of North Carolina State University wrote that the ratio of coyote to wolf to dog DNA changes regionally; northeastern coyotes have more coyote DNA than dog, while mid-Atlantic coyotes have more dog DNA than wolf. Hybridization occurred generations ago, and there's no current evidence that eastern coyotes continue to breed with dogs or wolves. Whatever the recipe, the eastern coyote is larger than its western cousin, and they're adaptable as hell, appearing and denning in paved and busy places like downtown Chicago and Manhattan. They trot through neighborhoods at night and even in the broad daylight. A western desert writer would say Coyote Man is bold and sure-footed, and his trickster nature means he can appear in the bank parking lot one moment and vanish the next—rarely seen, never captured. But here in the east, they're just scarfing around in the trash.

That's not to say that the eastern coyotes are only dumpster divers. Coyotes are opportunistic hunters, first and foremost. They'll eat what they can get, whether it crawls, swims, flies, runs, or rots in a Hefty bag. No wonder nobody has written anything lyrical about them. The coyote on trash night, pawing through an empty lo mein carton doesn't shine quite as mystically as Coyote on a butte, howling out his ancestral song at the crescent moon. It's hard to elevate a creature to the revered status of Coyote Man when your coyotes aren't revered.

West Virginians revere deer. In 2021, 200,000 West Virginians sat in tree stands and under bushes and bagged over 100,000 whitetails. Deer have been hunted here for as long as humans have dwelled in the mountains, long before white settlers arrived. When they did, they hunted the whitetails into dangerously low numbers. Careful management, once implemented, gave the species the rebound it needed. Now, deer are so prevalent that many cities have a backyard hunt. In fact, I'm watching a doe, right now, nibbling the dried winter stalks of my hosta and pooping on my deck.

Our reverence for the whitetails has sustained many a rugged mountaineer family in times of food scarcity. It's brought generations together—parents and children, the latter of whom start early, before their tenth birthdays. Hunters contribute huge sums of money to conservation efforts in the state. And though we rage when deer nip the buds off our tuberous begonias, they remain a tradition, a living hearth and home around which we gather, each winter.

The West Virginia Division of Natural Resources (DNR)'s efforts to restore the deer population culminated in the 1990s, when numbers were at their highest. Since then, whitetails have been in a managed decline with the department's steady hand on the wheel.

As boots-on-the-ground witnesses, hunters provide the DNR with reports from the field. But this is where things start to go off the rails, because the tradition of blaming the eastern coyote for a poor deer harvest and shrinking numbers is just as ingrained. In fact, finger pointing has become routine, as has the paranoia that rises whenever a coyote is spotted in an urban area.

In my experience, West Virginians feel strongly about coyotes, few of them positively. We fear and despise them because a tradition of misinformation follows the canids. The moment someone spots one, the whole neighborhood rises up in social media hysteria.

*Get your family inside! They're coming for your kids!* Someone posts on a neighborhood Facebook page that there's a pack, twenty animals strong, running around with fangs bared, snatching toddlers right out of their sandboxes. Someone else reports screams and howls in the night. Unconfirmed advisories, supposedly from city officials, warn that snarling death is on the prowl and to lock up the dogs, cats, chickens, and petite mothers-in-law.

It all seemed unnecessarily intense to me, and I watched this repetitive discourse for years until one day I could stand it no longer and decided to write an informative article, for which I called Rich Rogers, who was then the DNR's furbearer biologist.

"A lot of people think coyotes are killing all the deer," Rogers told me. "That's just not true. Deer densities have been declining now for a number of years, mainly due to high antlerless harvests, which is what we wanted. We wanted to get these deer densities down close to the carrying capacity. They were way over for a number of years." He also said deer rely on brushy land and trees in early stages of development for food, and since there's not as much timber cutting as there used to be, these areas aren't as ubiquitous.

Coyotes do prey upon fawns, as do bears and bobcats. In June and July, a coyote's diet consists of 70 percent fawns. That said, a recent Pennsylvania study looked at fawn mortality, and while fawns die from predation (black bears kill more than coyotes), it doesn't reduce the deer population. To be certain, biologists repeated the study and got the

Pure, Unadulterated Garbage

same results. The University of Delaware conducted a separate study on fawn mortality in 2018. Coyotes, bears, and bobcats do not exist in Delaware, but that state's rate of fawn deaths was the same as West Virginia's and Pennsylvania's.

"Everything kills fawns," Rogers said, adding that he's even seen a mink kill a fawn. Starvation is very common, too.

The coyote's reputation as a killer was not helped by a PBS documentary called *Meet the Coywolf.*

"That was pure, unadulterated garbage," Rogers said. "And that caused such a stir, that program, with people thinking, 'Oh my gosh, we've got this elite predator on the loose!' That's not true. Absolutely not true. Coyotes aren't elite predators."

He said there are not as many coyotes in West Virginia's northern panhandle—where I live—as we think there are. In fact, the number living in Marshall, Ohio, Brooke, and Hancock Counties combined is only around 260 animals. The intensity of the nightly coyote chorus—being heard closer and closer to suburbia—makes that figure hard to believe, but Rogers said those yips and screams come from only four or five animals. Coyotes don't live in packs; it's a family group consisting of two monogamous parents and their young, whose chances of survival are poor. Half of the pups die every year, and most never make it to age four.

He's also heard the rumor that various state divisions introduced coyotes to control the deer population, a common refrain grumbled out the side of an aggrieved deer hunter's mouth.

"That is a provincial myth," he said. "No state has ever introduced coyotes. Over the past thirty-four years, I have had many people tell me that they have proof of such, and I have yet to be provided with any. I can confidently say the same of all my colleagues in every northeast and southeast state."

Once I'd spoken to Rogers, I wrote the article and, with hopeful naivete firmly intact, waited for people to read the truth about coyotes and welcome science into their hearts.

I couldn't have gotten a chillier reception if I'd shown up at Thanksgiving with a PETA shirt and a gelatinous Tofurky. The comments online were, in hindsight, perfectly predictable. And poorly punctuated.

*They will trick your pets away from the house and eat them they will go after small children. Be careful.*

*They can also scale eight-foot fences. Grab your pet and go.*

*They are cunning. I have heard stories they will take the dogs squeaky toy and run off to the edge of the woods squeak it and lure your dog out where other coyote are waiting.*

Stories. Someone has always heard a story, from his brother, from his brother-in-law, from his brother-in-law's friend Skeeter who has three DUIs and is facing a misdemeanor charge of indecent exposure but is definitely credible. And while you might wonder why the coyote would bother with the toy when it could just snatch the little dog right there in the yard, it's best not to bring that up in the comment section on a West Virginia Facebook page, because obstinate folks get defensive and call you bad names. (Normally I take "Hippie tree hugger" as a compliment, but when it's paired with the word "crackpot," it loses some of its warm fuzzies.)

The comments proved exactly what Rogers told me, that people had already made up their minds. It's called confirmation bias. Those who believe in a certain answer or outcome will look for evidence to support it, even when presented with conflicting facts. When we note the declining deer population (or a missing cat), and then see or hear a family of coyotes in the area, we automatically connect the two. But correlation does not equal causation.

Coyotes are opportunists, first and foremost. They will indeed grab a domestic feline if they can. In 2007, an unusually chill coyote walked into a downtown Chicago Quiznos and made himself at home in the freezer. Chicago has a notable urban coyote population, and while the animals lie low and avoid people, they're increasingly drawn to easy meals and garbage. That's when they encounter humans. And, as any student of the Anthropocene knows by now, those interactions never end well. They're understandably defensive of their young and will attack a free-roaming dog to protect their pups. Internet videos prove that a lone coyote can indeed go after a little kid.

"The survivors from the previous year's litter take off looking for home ranges that they can occupy, and that's what causes a lot of problems—transient animals," Rogers told me. "It's like taking a bunch of sixteen- and seventeen-year-olds and kicking them out of the house. What do they do? Get in trouble."

Encounters are usually attributable to our habits: We've left pet food out and offered them regular meals. Or we've encroached on their territory, developed land where a coyote family lives, and pushed the animals out of their habitat. Rogers didn't deny that attacks have happened, though they're incredibly rare—the Humane Society of the United States reports that more people are killed each year by errant golf balls and champagne corks than coyotes.

Nevertheless, my article's comment section grew rough and rowdy. Had I been there in person, I would've been targeted with rotting vegetable matter for my blasphemy. I learned, as Rich Rogers warned me, that minds don't change easily. Sadly, he died in 2022 after thirty-seven years with the DNR. I'd have other interviews with him before his passing, and he was a warm source of knowledge and a consummate West Virginia outdoorsman. I wish he was still out there because, as the minor flap about my article died down, I felt I'd lost the battle. I'd drawn my sword one hundred years too late.

And so, while the western coyote leads his followers through the desert, over the slickrock, and along the line between ecology and folklore, the eastern coyote will always be a varmint. He's too skulking to be majestic and wild, too adaptable to be anything but a toddler-terrorizing, cat-snatching villain. What might look like wisdom in the surefooted canine as he slips through a dusty arroyo looks more like a plot to scarf a bowl of Fancy Feast when he's creeping along Greenwood Avenue. No writer has seized upon the eastern coyote with reverence. Nobody is following a lyrical trickster's trail of mischief through Wheeling, West Virginia.

Odds are good, though, that he's following ours.

# Finding My People

I f you happen to be driving through the heart of West Virginia—and by that, I mean the geographic center of the state—you'll find yourself puttering through the small towns of Flatwoods and Sutton. There's an outlet mall where you can buy Fiestaware (a colorful West Virginia export that draws plate-loving pilgrims from the far corners of the world), sit in several oversized chairs shaped like the famous Flatwoods Monster, and visit a museum dedicated to that particular cryptid. There's also a hotel and convention center where I attended a West Virginia Writers board meeting one September.

West Virginia Writers is the largest writers' organization in the state. They work to promote writing and West Virginia authors, and they gather every June for a conference in Ripley. I was still relatively new to the organization, and I'd volunteered to be the northern panhandle's regional representative. The state's other regional reps and I were to meet in the hotel lobby and join the board for our part of the session.

I hadn't met any of the other reps, but it would be easy enough to find them. After all, writers aren't hard to spot. In any room, seek out the corner-lurkers, the ones with sweeping eyes who look like they've been wearing someone else's pants all day but only just realized it. Writers are gregarious and often giddy amongst each other, but alone, they stand back and study whatever's going on. (Think Sir David Attenborough in the Tanzanian bush, but with a latte rather than a spotting scope.) You're far more likely to see a writer in that situation than the way they're portrayed in Hollywood movies—mildewing in a spartan attic apartment with nothing more than a bed and typewriter. That's all wrong. Writers can't have a bed in our writing area because we'll choose sleep over writing every time. Spartan is inaccurate because it doesn't account for the four mismatched bookcases, seventeen anthologies on the nightstand, nine leather journals we can't bring ourselves to write in, and the three empty mugs with moldy tea bags on the desk. And of course, the butt pillow, for gluteal support. The typewriter, however, is the most laughable element of these scenes. No writer uses them because you can't procrastinate on a typewriter. You can't switch over to another window or tab. And if you think I haven't checked Facebook eight times over the course of the last paragraph and Googled whether Mothra's larval form could defeat Rodan if they battled underwater, you're putting way too much faith in my work ethic.

What movies do get right is the general oddness of the writer. When you look at one, holed up in a coffee shop, you can't decide if they're painfully introverted or simply composing a haiku about the way you just tripped on the carpet and pretended you did it on purpose. (The answer is both. And rest assured—the writer tripped on the same rug five minutes ago, said, "Fuck!" in front of a six-year-old, and fell into a trash can.) In a crowd or party, writers can sniff each other out by their mannerisms, which often reveal a blend of intrigue and terror, glazed with a light coat of self-loathing. They are, however, always studying their surroundings—namely the people, and it's an addictive habit. Everything they see goes into the creative pot, to be drawn from in an essay or story down the road. The human condition fascinates them; they digest interactions, ruminate over them, chew on them until they break down, and spit them back out onto paper. Writers are basically llamas with a laptop and a nagging case of impostor syndrome.

Thus, given my knowledge of myself, I was sure I could find the other West Virginia Writers regional representatives, as we were supposed to meet down in the lobby at ten and proceed up to the conference room. At 9:55, I wandered into the conference center lobby, where I was sure to find my people. They'd be sitting in comfortable chairs, coffee mugs in hand, notebooks ready. We'd settle in and chat about the summer conference and what we were writing and what we were reading.

To that end, West Virginia has no shortage of great writers. Pearl S. Buck, Homer Hickam, Irene McKinney, Breece D'J Pancake, Rebecca Harding Davis, Ann Pancake, Jeanette Walls. Many of them rose from humble beginnings, some from poverty.

Appalachian writers are expected to write about our mountain culture. About our childhood struggles, our grandparents—who never did get indoor plumbing—and the traditions of mining, hunting, and cooking up a mess of ramps and taters on Sundays. There's no shortage of creative works—of all genres—that dwell in this realm. Of late, however, a new chorus of voices is rising from West Virginia—queer voices, voices of color, and the literary community is eager for it.

But our West Virginian-ness still clings to us, and it's just off-putting enough to make us stand out. This is a weird state, backward and infuriating and stricken with addiction, obesity, and poverty. Everyone knows it—we, most of all. And yet, in the synergy of heart and heartbreak, of pain and peace, we find ourselves tethered, by our roots, our genes, and by this place, to something even a writer cannot always find the words to describe.

The author, Matthew Neill Null, wrote a 2016 *LitHub* essay recalling an encounter with a poet while living in the rural South. He said he liked it there, in the poet's neck of the woods, but she asked him how he could stand "all those fucking rednecks."

"Well," Null wrote, "those fucking rednecks are my people." He didn't say it out loud, though, knowing it was pointless. It's a sentiment West Virginians feel in our bones because oddities and the extremes always claim the spotlight and we have both, here. In a prime example, Null points out that there are 136,000 Methodists in West Virginia (including me, once upon a Sunday long past), but the handful of snake-handling churches make a far better subject, especially in the eyes of a publisher. J.D. Vance's memoir of his abusive, alcoholic family offers a lurid look—what some call "poverty porn"—at Appalachia, one with a sharper hook than the ubiquitous I-grew-up-poor-but-I-survived memoir. It's irritating, because sensational stories might get publishing deals and grab headlines, but they're not always us.

Null's *LitHub* essay is titled "No One is Writing the Real West Virginia."

"Few places can rival its beauty and the friendliness, toughness, and humility of its people," he writes. "A place of silence, it forces one to turn inward." Certainly, Appalachia has its share of ugliness, of desperation. Ours may seem like a miserable existence, and it can be. Sometimes the written accounts and the realities of growing up here are so overwhelming that readers from other places may miss the hope woven through each page, each story.

But it's there.

At the Days Inn in Flatwoods, I wandered down the hotel corridors, toward the lobby. I was looking forward to finding my people. Reuniting. My nascent literary connections had yet to grow into a writing family, and I was excited by the prospect.

When I emerged from the hallway, I did see people. Everywhere. They filled the lobby and gathered around tables set up outside the event room, which flickered with activity. I'd stumbled into a convention of some sort, and the crowd was largely male. People flowed in through the automatic doors from the parking lot, striding with purpose toward the tables where other people with badges checked them in. I spotted a circle of comfortable chairs in the far corner and headed for them, but I had to cross the stream of event-goers to get there. As I picked my way through the busyness, my shoulder clipped an older gentleman. He wore a checked shirt, jeans, and a US Navy ball cap. We both stopped, and I said, "Oh, I'm sorry, excuse me."

"Pardon me, ma'am," he said, and paused with his arm out, offering me the right of way. But it wasn't the gesture of his left hand that caught my eye. It was the gun he held in his right.

"Uh, thanks," I said. He smiled and walked toward the check-in tables, falling into line behind several other men. The guy in front of him gripped a pistol. The guy in front of that one clutched a shotgun. The lady in front of him wore a hot pink holster studded with rhinestones. Whatever she held in her hand was also pink. In the corner, on a chair upholstered in a floral print, a man dozed, chin against chest, a rifle draped across his lap. Groups of old friends found each other and gathered in tight circles, talking with weapons in hand.

These were not my people.

For the record, it's not always hard to find your people. Some of us are born into our people and fit naturally into our families. Others—those we refer to as black sheep—know from a very young age that their blood relations break down beyond chromosomal similarities. These are the folks that have to find their people in the world, and it's complicated because who your people are changes with age and maturation. My high school friends are mostly strangers now; my college friends have scattered, too, and the thing that linked us in time and space—our chosen university—no longer holds any magnetic pull.

I tried on many different lifestyles and groups and relationships in my twenties and thirties, and all of them withered. It wasn't until I went back to school for creative writing that I found a label, a role, and a place that fit. It's where I found my people. They were readers and writers and poets. They were gregarious and shy and determined and nutty. They were international, academics, and Appalachians. I recognized each of their gifts—to the world, to the state, and to me, as friends and surrogate siblings. When I finally knew what to look for, I could find my people in a crowd.

And none of them were in that lobby.

Unlike many West Virginians, I know nothing whatsoever about guns. I can't tell you the difference between a Ruger and a Luger, which kind of rifle is for squirrels and which is for turkey. Nor did I have the wherewithal in those moments to study the details of each gun, so you'll have to settle for vague descriptions of what I saw that day. Some were long, some were short. Some were shiny, and others had seen many hunting seasons. I took two discreet photos just to document my reality, but neither picture offers enough detail for me to identify any weapons.

I'm not alone. The average fiction writer's search history probably reveals how little they know about weapons. I've found several websites devoted to educating writers on guns, warning them that they keep confusing magazines and clips and that a single bullet won't launch a person through a wall. Writing about firearms, and about crime in general, usually requires enough research that the author may consider forewarning the FBI their internet searches are about to take a dark turn.

*How do you get a dead body to sink?*

*How do you pluck out an eyeball without staining an imported silk tie?*

*How long would it take a wire fox terrier to eat a 164-pound man?*

Plenty of writers are gun owners. After all, West Virginia is full of huntable, edible varmints. If you want to shoot something and turn it into jerky, you're in the right place. But for those of us who don't, writing coaches might recommend going to the firing range and putting our hands on a gun so we can get a better sense of how to describe it. I've held and shot a gun one time in my life, and it wasn't for me. In a quirky state of outliers, I guess I'm an outlier.

Back in the hotel lobby, I settled into a chair in the corner, feeling like the only clothed person at a nude pool party. To everyone else, this was totally normal—just another gun show on a fall Saturday. Everybody was safe, everybody was friendly; this was a gathering of like-minded folks. All five hundred of them, and me, the only unarmed West Virginian in the lobby of the Days Inn & Suites by Wyndham Sutton Flatwoods.

Fortunately, the contrast between what I had been expecting—poets and writers—and what I found was so great that when a fellow West Virginia Writer, Brad, did walk through the door, I spotted him at once. It wasn't the absence of a firearm that gave him away; it was his expression. His eyes darted back and forth. For a few seconds he stood there, as shocked as I had been, and then he spotted me in a chair in the corner. My vaguely familiar face and awkward body position gave me away as one of his people, and he found his way over.

"Are we in the right place?" he asked, sinking into a chair, limb by limb.

"This is weird," I said and stared at the crowd that continued to stream in from the parking lot. One guy stood out. He looked as though he'd just walked into the ladies' room by accident. *These are not my people.*

It was Jørn. We waved at him to catch his attention, and for a second, he looked like a *Deadliest Catch* crewman that had fallen overboard into the Bering Sea and was tossed a lifeline.

"Are we in the right place?" he asked.

"This is weird," I said.

"This is weird," Brad said.

Then, Tom showed up. We fished him out of the crowd, too, followed by Lisa, who we discovered in a second, quieter lobby. We huddled together in a tight ball—the way baitfish do when they're surrounded by sharks—as we went upstairs to the board meeting, which had been going on for several hours. Insulated from the rest of the hotel in a snug conference room, the board members had no idea what was going on downstairs. We told them about the experience we'd all had, together, finding ourselves so unexpectedly out of place. It was a bizarre commonality to share with strangers, and yet it was that out-of-place discomfort that turned us into friends.

People.

Every June, those friends and I gather in Ripley for the annual West Virginia Writers conference. We speak, we teach, we listen, we learn. But most of all, we reunite as literary family with the shared knowledge that there's something different about writers, here in the Mountain State. The conference is a safe space, a few moments when we're reminded that we aren't the only awkward, anxious weirdos wandering through the hollows, scrambling to capture moments of beauty that might otherwise get us laughed out of a roadside diner or at least regarded with a lifted eyebrow. Our love of home is as strong as our love of words. We share the simplest bond: we're from West-by-God Virginia. That alone links us in time and space and adds an element to our gatherings I've never felt anywhere else. Here we are, struggling to explain determination in a life of hardship and a place of sorrow. Here we are, describing mountains that sit low and silent and old and worn, crinkles of ground down rock that have lived many lives in many ages, trying to explain their gravity while not fully understanding it ourselves. Here we are, poring over words that explain why we stay in West Virginia, even though we wake up many days wishing to be anywhere else.

How do you categorize that ambivalence? How do you explain nonsense? How do you convey sorrowful hope and hopeful sorrow? Writers in this place don't know, but we try nonetheless, generation after generation.

Irene McKinney, the poet laureate of West Virginia from 1994 to 2012 said, "When people say this state is backward, I simply am astounded. I had access to a farm community, a small peaceful town and school and good, dedicated teachers. I was in nature and in literature—a perfect combination for a writer." Faced with enough pushback and scornful pity, we all eventually learn to let go our attempts to contradict any of it. McKinney also said, "I'm a hillbilly, a woman, and a poet, and I understood early on that no one was gonna listen to what I had to say anyway so I might as well say what I want to."

The great writers who emerged from this state shared this connection, to each other and to the words of Appalachia. They also knew, as we do, that the fog of our state's reputation hangs over everything we are and everything we write.

That doesn't mean we're living in the fog, though. As writers, we know it's our job, not only to tell our stories, but to tell the stories of those who came before us, who never had a turn at the microphone. That's quite a responsibility, and when we allow ourselves to feel its weight, a privilege can easily feel like a mantle. Surely, it's not the writers' job to change the world's view on hillbillies. To combat stereotypes. To give voice to the voiceless, the uneducated, the addicted, and the poor.

But, if not us, who? Appalachian writers have a foot in two worlds: the world of language, of literature; and the world where we're looked down upon simply because of our area code. It doesn't matter that the last three letters of your name are "PhD" if the first three numbers are 304.

We defend our home ferociously, but we've also learned over time that the way to change hearts and minds isn't to fly at readers' heads in rage and disgust. It does no good to argue; it does no good to present facts (especially now, when facts no longer hold the weight they once did). The way to readers' hearts is through narrative. It's a lot harder to keep us at bay when you've read about the families swept away in the Buffalo Creek flood or the determined child who grew up picking stray pieces of coal around the tipple with her father so they'd be able to stay warm at night. (FYI: That's West Virginia writer Katherine P. Manley's *Don't Tell'em You're Cold*.) You might also find yourself sucked into Null's account of the guy who went to court because someone sold him a coonhound that refused to bark, chased deer instead of raccoons, and, when presented before the jury, lifted his leg on the American flag.

"We straddled both worlds," Null wrote of West Virginians in a *Paris Review* essay, "enjoying our brick homes and security but never quite sure where we fit into the scheme, so we laughed at ourselves, which was acceptable." West Virginians get it; West Virginia writers get something more. And no matter how fruitless our attempts to reshape the trope may feel, we'll continue to do so.

Our anecdotes from the Flatwoods gun show never spread, because we didn't really share them, in part because it didn't seem like such a big deal in hindsight, but also because it would have been hard to convey the bizarre abruptness of those moments and the long seconds when we felt so untethered among the people—West Virginians—to whom we'd normally gravitate out in the wider world, the people we'd call "ours." We did straddle both worlds, and worlds within worlds. And maybe everyone in that hotel would all look the same to a New York eye or through a California gaze. Indeed, we *would* all be the same, because we'd share statehood and the lived experiences of our brethren, those with whom we shared DNA or an area code or an oddly shaped plot of backward terrain wedged between Ohio and Virginia. We honor that sameness and grasp those hands when we meet, whether they hold a rifle or a pen.

But when those of us who were there that day meet each other out in any of these worlds, or at the annual conference, we sometimes recall that weird and uncomfortable morning, the convergence of in-place and out-of-place, and a curious irony that made us feel so strangely alone and yet so wholly understood.

# Dear Richwood

However you might envision the event Richwood, West Virginia, calls "the grandaddy of all ramp festivals," you're probably picturing it wrong. I certainly was. When I imagined the event, I saw closed off streets and people squeezing into artisan tents, fiddle and banjo floating over the crowd, kettle corn and fried things. And I imagined the ramp dinner: a town coming together in a great hall, brilliantly lit, the tables accented with the vibrant colors of the mountains.

That wasn't what I found.

I'd spent a decade trying to get to the famous Feast of the Ramson. While ramps grow in the northern panhandle of West Virginia, where I live, their arrival isn't heralded with quite as much fanfare or reverence as it is in the mountains. We love them, to be sure, but the deeper into the state you travel, the larger ramps grow in the hearts and forests of West Virginians, and the more annual ramp dinners you'll find. I wanted so much to attend the Feast, but every year, some obstacle barred my way: bad weather, sick kids, and COVID-19. And each year I missed it, the event grew in my mind.

Ramps are reborn annually, the first green that peers out from beneath winter's long decay. Foragers anticipate their emergence and the ramp dinners that will pop up in VFWs and church basements. Ramp feasts are sacred. Women of the town and church tend the muggy kitchens as their husbands, damp with sweat, haul fresh ramps in boxes, slice cornbread baked in parishioners' homes the night before, and pour sassafras tea.

Ramps range from Georgia to Canada, so West Virginia lays no official claim to them. But foraging is a part of our culture, and ramps—weird and delicious—fit our state's unique character. They're not a delicacy, here. They're simply tradition.

In *Reekin' Ramp Recipes*, author and ramp connoisseur Barbara Beury McCallum writes, "The late great West Virginia writer Jim Comstock had this to say about the ramp: 'A ramp is just an onion that hasn't been civilized or had the fear of the Lord driven into it; it's Nature's best evidence that He who made the lamb also made the tiger."

Ramps are hard to categorize. They look like an onion, taste stronger than a leek, and smell more garlicky than a scallion. But these alliums aren't a composite character, a sum of parts. They belong, simply, to spring. They're wild, stinky, and worshipped.

Everything fell into place in 2021. The trip was on. For weeks I watched the Feast of the Ramson's Facebook event page. The preparation committee called for volunteers to help with the tedious cleaning process—removing the bulbs' grimy membranes, snipping the roots, and washing away the soil without damaging the emerald leaves.

We arrived in Webster Springs—one county away and the only lodging I could find—the night before the festival. It took several hours, hundreds of curves in the road, and a heavy dose of Dramamine for ten-year-old Ben. Most of the town had closed, but we wandered into a local meat shop and talked ramps with the owners. We told them how we liked ours: grilled with olive oil and cracked pepper. Ramp burgers. Ramp pesto. Ramp chimichurri on lamb chops with a hint of mint.

They grinned and said, "We just cook 'em in bacon grease."

Regardless of how you prepare them, a group of ramps is called a mess, like a clowder of cats or a bellowing of bullfinches. Ramps may sell for twenty dollars per pound at farmers' markets. Famous chefs rave about them. Ramp season is limited to a few weeks in the spring, which adds to their mystique and cost. Unfortunately, in many states, ramp populations have been decimated by irresponsible and unsustainable foraging. Seeds take six to eighteen months to germinate; plants take five to seven years to reach reproductive maturity. Ramps are protected in Quebec; Great Smoky Mountain National Park outlawed the harvest; Maine and Rhode Island designated them a species of concern. In 2022, the National Park Service disallowed the ramp harvest in West Virginia's New River Gorge National Park. Surveys reveal an alarming decline. It's why many West Virginians keep their patches secret.

Ramp dishes can be as complicated or as simple as you like. The ramp can work with you. It's flexible, forgiving. The ramp's intensity depends on how you cook it, but it's not a first-date kind of meal. I didn't know how the ramps would be presented at the Feast of the Ramson—I

Deep & Wild

just wanted to be there, at the world's greatest ramp festival, in the state I loved so much.

Richwood looked nothing like I'd imagined, but it checked off every box on the list of small-town West Virginia characteristics. Quaint main street with a few hippie shops and several shuttered buildings. Houses built into the side of the hill. Trout stream behind the Walgreens, stocked with rainbows.

In the parking lot between the fire house and the public library, ten or so blue pop-up tents and tables had been erected and populated with colorful things I couldn't identify from a distance but could easily guess: T-shirts, wood crafts, candles. Shiplap signs. A thin crowd meandered about, and I wondered aloud if we'd come too early. We parked behind a flat patch of sod where a man sat with a guitar on his lap, inaudibly plucking strings. Was this the Appalachian music promised on the flier? Where was the banjo? The bluegrass? I spotted a fiddle, but it spent most of the afternoon in the grip of an older gentleman who stuck to timeless classics like "Twinkle, Twinkle Little Star" and "Mary Had a Little Lamb."

A painted sign that said RAMP FEED pointed to the Moose Lodge, the heart of the festival. The feast. People formed a line at the entrance; it stretched halfway across the lot.

"Looks like a half-hour wait," I said. Following the other event-goers (I decided this no longer qualified as an actual festival), we crossed the road and took our place. Soon, the line curved to keep people out of the street. The couple in front of us, from Harper's Ferry, had driven a long way, too. The couple behind us—locals—handed out invitations for an upcoming church picnic. I picked a ladybug off a woman's back as she reminded her partner how patient she was being. She told me she'd buy my book. I said I had to write it first. Ben found a shady wall to sit on and watched us inch forward from beneath his Dramamine-heavy eyelids.

"The line inside is twice as long," came a voice as we stepped up to the door after forty-five minutes in the sun.

"What?" the ladybug woman shouted.

"He's kidding," I said.

He was not kidding. It was like an amusement park ride, the kind with an outdoor line and an indoor line. When you finally reach the

**Dear Richwood** 75

door, you're so excited—you waited, didn't complain, and now, finally, it's time. And then your eyes adjust, and you see a maze of turnstiles and a line of humans resentfully crammed together because they, too, were fooled into thinking it was their turn.

Ben couldn't handle it. He didn't care about ramps. I sent him to a chair with my phone, where he held YouTube up to his ear to pass the time. I talked to a guy with the Penn State Extension about a ramp survey. Blood pooled in my lower body, and I felt a hemorrhoid coming on. Ninety minutes in, we finally saw the dining room and people eating. We heard women chattering in the kitchen, metal serving spoons scraping against chafing dishes, and the hiss of soda cans cracking open as ramp-eaters found their seats.

A full two hours after we'd taken our place in line, we rounded the final corner, and it was before us. The ramp spread. The dinner I'd been dreaming about for a decade. Would it be ramps and potatoes? Would it be ramp pasta? Would it be grilled ramps, flashing red and green against an ivory plate?

"What is *that*?" Ben blurted, pointing at the serving dishes. I recognized ham, fried potatoes, and brown, caramelized beans. I saw fresh cornbread, cake slices, and golden, sticky pie. But he was pointing to a chafing dish piled with dark, wet leaves and pale bulbs. There they were, not dressed in olive oil or smeared on lamb chops but softened in their own liquid and, no doubt, a helping of bacon grease. The dish was pure ramps, cooked in their most basic form, an artery between wild and domestic, forest and human.

Disappointment hit hard. We could have prepared the same meal at home—we had our own ramps in the fridge. But I didn't want the West Virginians who'd been foraging and cleaning and preparing for weeks—with Christian love—to see anything but our gratitude, so we held out our arms and accepted their offerings with thank-you's and these-look-wonderful's and stumbled out into the April sunlight to find a table.

Ben sat down under an umbrella, clutching a Mountain Dew as he nibbled a fistful of warm cornbread. Crumbs tumbled down his shirt. He poked at the ramps, proclaimed them "delicious," and left most of them on his plate, hoping we wouldn't notice. My husband and I made exuberant declarations of hunger to cover up the fact that the ramps weren't what we'd expected. But they'd been tended with joy by devout volunteers, from harvest to plate. Our unspoken, emotional conflict hovered over the table.

We ate. And just as Richwood and the feast were packaged differently than I'd imagined, so were the ramps. In the gentle care of the preparers, pungent garlic had melted into softness, to warmth. They weren't stinky, as our ramps at home tended to turn out; they were rich and savory. They tasted like the dishes aunts and grandmothers brought to Easter dinner, the meals that triggered an afternoon nap. They tasted like the days between winter and spring. They were flavors I'd never achieved in my own kitchen. I sat with them as the multitudes streamed out of the hall, plates balanced in their arms. Old hands grasped small ones, leading a new generation into tradition. Families greeted each other and offered brief but earnest prayers over Styrofoam plates.

*This* was the Feast of the Ramson.

On our way out of town, we stopped along the Cherry River, a classic West Virginia trout stream, cold and clear and dotted with boulders. I perched on one, above a deep pool, and watched a trio of trout hover in the current, waving their tails as they waited for a meal of their own. Ben sat nearby, rolling small stones into the water and listening to them *plunk*. We were full and quiet, and I mumbled something about making it an annual pilgrimage.

Whether or not we return, the annual observance will go on in Richwood, and while few West Virginians would openly identify as nature worshippers, the land here is rich with spirit. The April communion of mountain and forest is laid out before the muddy boots of foragers. By coincidence—or not at all—ramps appear at Easter time, a movable feast that's born again each year, tended and attended by Richwood's faithful for eighty-three years. As promised, the body of Christ is not broken but resurrected. The ramps will return, if we offer them our care, and the line of ramp seekers that day revealed the depth of Richwood's devotion to the season's promised blessing.

I didn't share the beliefs of the ramp-eaters around me—I'm a pagan, a nature worshipper who withdrew from Christianity some time ago. I find no comfort in the white linens and colored glass of a sanctuary; my god lives in the mountains. She *is* the mountains, the tumbling rivers, the red spruce. Her body, the sacred green folds of the West Virginia landscape, is the only place I find peace in this world, and I admit I felt removed from the churchgoers around me in line, as though I stood out, a heathen among saints. The mountainous walls of earth rose above the town of Richwood, and the yellow-green curtain of spring closed around the forested slopes, where the ramps grew. Whatever else lived behind it was a mystery, wild and tempting.

Richwood sits deep within the state, tucked up against the Cranberry Wilderness. There's no easy way to get there, no direct path or level road. Surrounded by miles of twisting topography, the rest of the world feels removed and inaccessible. It's a journey to reach Richwood and a journey to find your way home.

My father used to tell me that life was about journeys, not destinations.

The day I went to Richwood, I missed the meaning of the celebration, and it took me a year to understand why. I'd gone for the wrong reasons, put too much emphasis on the word *festival* and not enough on *feast*. The parking lot sign and the event page were clear: it was a ramp *feed*, not a carnival. The Feast of the Ramson is a ritual of thanks and renewal. And when my doubt and disappointment threatened to darken the experience, I met an unexpected love of neighbor, community, and nature.

It was the most West Virginia moment of my life. Only here do you arrive at the ramp capital of the world, for the festival of all festivals and find a solitary fiddle and a line at the Moose. Only here do you meet a group of people who spend a season preparing to feed neighbors and friends. Only here do they offer this communion to strangers, to those who don't believe, and to those who don't yet understand. Only here, in West Virginia, does a stinky little leek hold so much hope.

Deep & Wild

# Blink, Chirp, Buzz: A West Virginia Invertebrate Index

W e don't call the bugs with the glowing butts "fireflies" in West Virginia. We call them lightning bugs. When I was young, the neighbor kids and I waited for them each evening under humid, purple skies, the June grass soft on our bare feet. The first tentative lights winked on in the blooming peonies, and as the darkness descended, a bioluminescent symphony overtook the yard. We caught them, studied them, and released them. For injured individuals with a misshapen wing or a broken antenna, we created Lightning Bug Regional Hospital, a level one trauma center and skilled rehab facility. Managed by four seven-year-olds, routine insect care consisted of petting them and offering a pep talk: "It's okay, lightning bug. I'll squeeze you tight and love you until you're all better! Let's practice flying. Try to take off. Oh, you fell!"

Our success rate with firefly rehab was depressingly low. It's hard to imagine how a fumbling set of fingers and a heart full of obsessive love could possibly go wrong, but somehow, the more we caught, the more patients had to be admitted to our facility, which really should have been called Lightning Bug Memorial Hospital. Eventually, the CEO—my dad—stepped in and shut us down. Something about ethical violations.

Researchers believe that lightning bugs developed their ability to light up as a warning; the bioluminescent chemical reaction signals their distastefulness to predators. Over time, however, it also became a way to attract a mate. Females sit on the ground and watch the flying males' flashes. When they see a display they like (the brighter and flashier the better), the females signal in return and a match is made.

But it's not always that simple. Though the annual lightning bug dating event appears sweet and joyful to us, down on the ground, there's drama playing out between two genera: *Photinus* and *Photuris*. (Think Romulus and Remus but without the hills or the cities or the complicated mythology. Also, they're beetles.) As the *Photinus* males fly around and signal for mates, predatory *Photuris* females lurk in the grass and assume a false identity to lure the *Photinus* males in. *Photuris* females have learned to mimic the flashing patterns of *Photinus* females. It's firefly catfishing. Just when an eager *Photinus* fellow thinks he's found his soulmate, she tackles and devours him. They do this to absorb defensive compounds—the kind that make them taste terrible to a predator—from *Photinus* for their own protection and can pass the beneficial toxin on to their offspring. Scientists call the *Photuris* females "femme fatale fireflies." In response, some *Photinus* males have caught on and are developing their own bioluminescent tricks to counter the *Photuris* females' deception. A male may flash a different, unrecognizable pattern or, in an all-too-familiar move, simply hit the road when he realizes he's not going to get lucky.

Despite their tough side, lightning bug populations are diminishing around the world. Ecologists attribute this decline to habitat destruction. Firefly larvae grow in moist and humid places like rotting wood, forest litter, and along bodies of water like ponds and marshes. As we continue to develop forested lands and wetlands, we're paving over their nurseries. Lawn pesticides and chemicals kill firefly larvae. In addition, the brighter we make our world at night, the harder it is for them to reproduce. Artificial lights blind them and throw their flashes out of sync. It helps to turn off garden and landscaping lights at night and draw the drapes after dark. This is good practice anyway because, quite frankly, we're all sick of watching you eat raw cookie dough in your underwear at eleven o'clock at night.

Lightning bugs don't stay long. They're here and gone in a month, but West Virginia has no shortage of personable invertebrates, and whether you seek them out or not, they'll likely find you. A cricket found me once, and he stayed in my car for nine days. I don't know how he got in there, but he hid beneath my seats, calling for a lady friend who would never appear. At first, I thought I was suffering from tinnitus. I laughed when I realized it was a cricket. They're supposed to be good luck, a signal of forthcoming wealth and prosperity. Who wouldn't want a bit of fortune riding along on the highway? I tried to find him, but crickets are tiny and evasive, and they shut up the minute you get close. I searched for twenty minutes, bashed my knee, wrenched my neck, and gave up. I figured he'd escape or expire.

82

He did neither. You'd think he might have stopped singing after a few days, but he hopped around the vehicle and continued to croon—a technique known as stridulation, accomplished by rubbing two specialized wings together—from the tops of the headrests and the depths of the storage compartments. And I had the privilege of hearing him, every day. Grocery store. *Chirp.* School drop-off. *Chirp.* Bank. *Chirp chirp.*

He said nothing when my husband and kids were in the car. I told them about him, that I couldn't catch him, and that it wasn't quite as funny as it had been at first. They nodded politely, and, at one point, my husband said, "Do you hear the cricket now, Laura?" Thus, the problem grew from an insect-in-car issue to a sweeping concern for Mom's well-being. Which was ridiculous, at first, but on day eight, I thought about driving through the car wash with open windows to flush him out. By day ten, he went silent, having either escaped or died at his post. To this day, I'm not sure my family believes it really happened.

Probably because it wasn't my first cricket incident. A year prior, a doctor had prescribed a drug for fibromyalgia. A non-opioid painkiller, it soothed the chronic pain that drives some folks to actual opioids. I was thrilled when, on the third day, I woke up without a neckache or stiffness.

The crickets began chirping in my head on the fifth day. At first, I only heard them during quiet moments, like when I lay down in bed. One cricket joined another, and they chirped in unison. The chorus grew louder and more unified until they surrounded me in a constant, pulsating whine of insect song. I heard it over the TV and dinner conversations. I heard it in the shower.

I checked the drug's potential side effects on the website. It listed drowsiness, dizziness, dry mouth, constipation, difficulty concentrating, and weight gain. It did not, however, mention crickets. Not that I expected crickets per se to be listed, but if it had said something like, "drowsiness, dizziness, dry mouth, bullfrogs, constipation, bugling elk, difficulty concentrating, humpback whale song, and weight gain," at least I would have known my auditory hallucinations were in the right taxonomic kingdom. As it was, I was left to wonder if it was real or not.

When you hear something that you're pretty sure only exists in your head, you face a moment of uncertainty and, inevitably, self-consciousness. It's a big risk to look around a room and ask the other parties if they hear "that noise," because you know there's a solid chance they'll look at you with expressions that wander from confusion (*What noise?*) to recognition (*Oh, she's hearing things again*) and eventually settle on pity (*She's been like this ever since she fell out of that golf cart. Poor thing.*). Then again, if you *don't* ask the room if they hear that noise, and it turns out they *do* hear it but are also too self-conscious to ask, then nobody acknowledges the fact that the carbon monoxide detector has been going off for half an hour. So, ultimately, it's better to ask the people around you if they hear the crickets, too.

My family didn't hear them, but they did give me a withering look and patted me on the hand. I stopped taking the medication. The pain came right back, and it took four months for the chirping to stop.

A year later, when that real cricket checked into my Nissan for an extended stay, they got the same looks on their faces.

"Hey Dad, Mom says the crickets are back."

"Oh God, here we go again," he said. "Honey, there are no crickets."

"Crick-*et*," I said. "There's a crick-*et*. One."

"You're taking that prescription again, aren't you?"

I'm hardly the first to deal with a cricket in an inconvenient spot. I know people who've accidentally released crickets meant for their pet lizard into their homes, which makes my single cricket seem pretty benign compared to an orchestra of them in the living room. (That's the technical term. You'd think it might be an "irritation" of crickets. Or a "shut the fuck up" of crickets. Nope. It's "orchestra.")

Historically, of course, the most dreaded insects do arrive in swarms. In biblical times, short-horned grasshoppers, aka the plague of locusts, blew in on the hand of God and ate their way through Egypt. Unfortunately, it wasn't the last locust plague, and while we don't really know where God stands on the issue, current evidence points to climate change as a likely contributor to modern invasions.

In the eastern US, one of the most notorious insect invasions is that of the periodical cicada. West Virginians tend to call them seventeen-year locusts. It's a misnomer, because while crickets and grasshoppers belong to the order Orthoptera, cicadas are Hemipterans, the "true bugs." They're known for their remarkable life cycles;

they spend thirteen or seventeen years underground, depending on the species, before emerging in one giant mass to molt, breed, and die. Cicadas have no defense other than to rise from the ground in phenomenal numbers—sometimes more than 1.5 million individuals in a single acre—and since no predator is *that* gluttonous, many survive. Researchers believe that because thirteen and seventeen are prime numbers, predators cannot synchronize their generations with the cicadas' emergence and possibly, that the fifteen separate broods are also prevented from hybridizing. Different broods emerge in their home territories at different times; Brood V emerged in the northern panhandle of West Virginia in 1982, 1999, and 2016.

I was three in the summer of '82, so I don't remember any of it, and I didn't come home from college when they returned in June of '99. By 2016, I'd been hearing their stories for thirty-seven years, how they waited quietly underground for almost two decades, emerged in unfathomable numbers, and sang in a deafening, one-hundred-decibel chorus. They flew everywhere, people warned me. They clung to shirts and hair. They sang all day, every day, for six weeks, and it wasn't the gentle, rhythmic whir that rises and falls when the annual August dog-day cicadas sing; it was an ongoing shriek that made sitting outside miserable.

I love nature in whatever form it presents itself, but this talk started to worry me as their emergence neared. Each day, six-year-old Ben and I lifted our garden pavers and watched the nymphs meander through shallow tunnels in the top layer of soil. The weather warmed, the weather cooled. Just when I thought they might appear, they didn't. It was like being in the dentist's chair waiting for a root canal—you hear the dentist milling around as he prepares for the procedure, and you sort of want him to come in and get it over with and you sort of want him to fall down a mine shaft.

Ultimately, it was the cicada movie that thawed my heart.

Filmmaker Samuel Orr, known for his skill with time-lapse photography, had put together a crowdfunding campaign a few years prior to support his documentary on the periodical cicadas called *Return of the Cicadas*, and the preview was online, still generating interest. He included full moon shots and extreme closeups that somehow made the insects' bizarre, five-eyed faces and crunchy bodies look vaguely canine. For some viewers, the cicadas lost the ick factor and became a moving and powerful example of the miracles of nature and evolution. And while some insect-haters never warmed up to the cicadas, Orr had stumbled upon a recipe for thawing the human heart: violins. His score was packed with them. As the cicadas climbed into the trees and transformed from nymph to winged adult, the strings swelled, and I teared up. When he zoomed in on the individuals with deformed wings, the ones who had no chance of survival, I blubbered. By the time they all died at the end of their short lives, I'd wiped my nose on my sleeve and eaten half a Whitman's sampler to get through the emotional ordeal. My anxiety melted, and when they finally poured out of our own ground in May, I rejoiced. As Orr wrote, it was "one of the greatest insect outbreaks on earth."

The cicadas fascinated my kids. We sat outside and watched them crawl up the trees, shed their exoskeletons, and unfurl their paper-thin wings. The boys played gently with the new adults, placing them on Matchbox cars and in the copilot seat of the Millennium Falcon, next to Chewie. They wore the cicadas on their ears and noses, and the cicadas, exhausted from metamorphosis and the first day of the end of their lives, obliged. For all the bugs knew, this was it: the climax of their existence. And if they were disappointed that they'd crawled around in the dirt for seventeen years, survived rodents and dog pee, and grew a sexy body for the beady-eyed ladies only to find themselves dangling from a six-year-old's left nostril, they were polite enough to keep it to themselves.

But the cicadas did sing. It was louder than I'd expected, and more arrived each day. They emerged and sang, followed by more, who emerged and sang, followed by more. They poured out of the ground for two weeks. Like buffet-goers, some came early, most came on time, and some straggled in at the last minute, and this stretched the whole event out into six weeks of cicadas. And unlike the dog-day cicadas that perch politely in their trees, Brood V flew around madcap and higgledy-piggledy. They buzzed our heads. They sat on our shoulders and squealed in our ears, and they were particularly attracted to the riding lawnmower. Every time I mowed, they dive-bombed my face and clung to my shirt, hoping to woo the giant, sexy Craftsman that purred in just the right timbre.

Our dog ate and barfed them up on my bedroom carpet every evening. And I've got a strong stomach, but when I saw the contents—rotten exoskeletal husks sprinkled with decaying red eyeballs—I barfed. And then Ben sympathy-barfed, in an act of intestinal solidarity.

They were loud as hell. Periodical cicadas' decibel level combined with their sheer numbers make them one of the loudest sounds in nature, landing on the auditory offense scale somewhere between a troop of howler monkeys and the 1883 eruption of Krakatoa. The males call to females with their tymbal organ—a ridged membrane on their abdomens that, when contracted, makes a *click*. The cicadas contract it up to 480 times per second, turning the single click into a continuous drone when it bounces off the human eardrum. An air sac in their abdomen amplifies the sound further, and they use their wings to direct it at the ladies. The chorus was deafening.

By July, the human population of West Virginia's northern panhandle was overstimulated, irritable, and disgusted. We'd watched the long days of the summer solstice from our air-conditioned living rooms. We couldn't sit outside. Most of us had lost some hearing, some people had eaten one—either by accident or on the heels of several Pabst Blue Ribbons—and a few unlucky souls had been molested by lecherous Hemipterans while trimming quarter round on the driveway with a buzzing miter saw. The whole thing started to stink. *They* started to stink, too. As the cicadas' life cycle wound down, their carcasses littered the ground and rotted in the midsummer humidity. The entire neighborhood became an homage to the inevitability of death and decay, the stains on my carpet a semi-digested memento mori even Stanley Steemer couldn't erase. So, while the cinematic weeping of stringed instruments was more than capable of dissolving nature lovers into sniveling snot bubbles, the phlegm flowed a lot more freely in the beginning, before we'd plucked periodical cicadas from our bras, beards, and vodka tonics.

And then they were gone. They passed on their genes and died—the only quiet thing they'd done as adults. The air cleared of song and scream and the ground of fetid funk. Newborn nymphs dropped out of the trees and burrowed back into the earth to wait out wars and presidents and our children's years at home.

We heard birds again, and katydids. We opened our doors and windows, fired up our barbecues, and invited friends to the deck. We said, *That was the worst! We've gotta move before they come back.* And then we forgot about them.

That was probably their plan all along.

# Intruder Alert

When Shawn woke me up the other night around one o'clock, I'd been in the middle of a dream about a raspberry cheesecake. One moment I was reaching for a fork, and the next, a jittery man stood over me.

"Laura!"

"What?" I grumbled.

"Get up!" he hissed. And then he disappeared.

I sleep with ointment in my eyes because they're chronically dry, so I was half-blind as I stumbled out of bed. I fell into a ficus; I stepped on the dog. My vision blurred, but in the hallway, I saw the outline of a man clutching a broom. And in the summer in West Virginia, that can mean only one thing.

Bat.

Most West Virginians have probably had a bat in their house at least once. *Myotis lucifugus*, the little brown bat, commonly roosts in eaves, dormers, and holes in roofs. At night they follow cool air currents outside to begin their hunting activities. But, when we turn on our air conditioners, we create false drafts. Sometimes, they get confused—often, it's a baby bat—and follow the wrong path into the house. This is why you're under the kitchen table with a laundry basket on your head every June.

Shawn and I had done this dance before. When we said our vows, we acknowledged better and worse, good health and bad, and agreed to love each other with or without money. But nobody said a damn thing about bats, and in hindsight, I think the minister should have. We should have vowed to love each other in the presence of flying mammals, through squeaky, pants-shitting terror at midnight, for rabies shots or not, with or without a tennis racket. Then, at least, we would have known what we were getting into in this old house of ours.

I've got a long history with bats. For forty years, they've been invading my summers and living in my roofs—it's unavoidable in an old house. There was the bat that slammed into the wall and landed in a paint bucket. Another entertained the cats for an evening as it fluttered down the hallway, and our ferrets caught one in the bathtub. They've swooped me in the shower and the bedroom. They've dive-bombed me in the kitchen and the foyer. They've hung on screens and draperies. One August night when I was fourteen, a bat flew into the bedroom, and I fled to the couch in the basement where a second one promptly flopped out of the woodstove and chattered at me.

Shawn, on the other hand, had never shared a domicile with anything wilder than a dog. I met him when we worked together at West Liberty University, in an old building with a leaky roof colonized by a horde of little brown bats. Occasionally one would find its way down into the offices. We'd all freak out and call campus security to remove it. During the early phases of our courtship, Shawn promised he would take over if campus security failed to report. There'd been one in the men's room, he claimed, and he'd set the "poor little guy" free. I thought it was adorable, and I married him a few years later. Not just for his bat bravery, of course—he was a great guy. But maybe a little bit for his bat bravery.

He moved in and my home became our home.

A year or so later, I found a young bat outside, hanging on the stone foundation. I was eight and a half months pregnant with our first son, and I looked like a human beanbag chair. The bones of my face had melted into a vague, potato shape, and if the moon had disappeared in the night, anyone who looked at me would have known exactly who ate it. I could barely walk, and the July heat wave had reduced me to an amorphous pile of belly, boobs, and butt.

I handed my husband a bucket.

"Here you go," I said, gesturing toward the bat on the wall.

"Wait," he said. "What are you asking me to do?"

I wedged myself into a lawn chair.

"I can't even see my ankles," I said. "Besides, you've done this before. Just put him in the bucket the way you did at work and drop him onto a bush."

Shawn stared at me for a long time. He inhaled, approached the wall, and raised the bucket to cover the bat. He shuffled his feet and began to dance around like a boxer, holding the bucket like a shield.

I could see him physically and mentally build himself up, and as he crossed some invisible threshold of proximity, his nerve failed him and he darted away, swatting madly at his ear as though the bat was clinging to it. Regrouping, he sprang toward the animal, swinging the bucket in the air, like a mace, at nothing whatsoever. He looked like a man being chased by a bumblebee. The bat, for its part, opened one eye, shuffled its wings, and went back to sleep. My husband continued to hop around, still a measurable three feet away, cursing himself and the creature. Finally, he dropped the bucket.

"What the hell was that?" I asked him. He didn't answer and sprinted into the house. But I saw his eyes: he was horrified. I thought I'd married a brave bat-warrior, and now he was hiding in the kitchen, pouring himself a double shot of Glenlivet and gagging into the sink.

"What am I supposed to do now?" I yelled. "This thing can't stay! And what was all that bravery crap when we were dating? You said you were a bat guy!" His eyes peered around the doorframe at me and then vanished, and I knew I was on my own. I was the size of a planet and on my own.

I wasn't feeling brave either, but I knew one of us had to deal with the bat. Working myself up into determination, I held the bucket and unconsciously mimicked my husband's dance as I placed the container on top of the animal and slid a file folder down over the opening. Inch by inch, I tipped the bucket back until the bat flopped into the bottom.

It chirped, and I screamed and threw the bucket, the file folder, and the animal at a hydrangea and stumbled back to the house on my fat feet. Later, Shawn apologized and told me he would definitely take care of the next bat that showed up.

I told him to go fuck himself.

That wasn't the last incident. Several years later, when Ben was four days old, a bat flopped out of his nursery curtains when I pulled them back at dawn. I screamed and bolted from the room with the baby, slamming the door behind me. Shawn came running. He scaled the stairs two at a time to reach us.

"What's the matter?" he yelled. "Are you okay?"

"BAT!" I shouted.

Shawn did an about-face and flew back down the stairs even faster.

"Good luck," he called over his shoulder, and, once again, I was alone with a flappy critter and, this time, a baby.

My abdomen was still stitched and sore from my second C-section, so I called my father. He arrived within minutes, and he didn't flinch as he entered Ben's room. He, too, had done this many times, and he greeted the bat with his predictable kindness as he raised the window. The bat circled a few times and flew out.

But our pediatrician did not appreciate that hippie-dippie, born-free shit—the animal should have been tested for rabies, he said at our visit that afternoon. Now we had a serious problem: Ben had spent the night with the bat in his room and there was no way to know if he'd been bitten; bat teeth are tiny and bites often go unnoticed. He needed the rabies vaccine, but was a baby of five days old enough to receive it? The doctor excused himself to call the American Academy of Pediatrics while we waited in the exam room in parental agony. The very idea of a newborn receiving rabies shots was a horror, even more so the idea that he might *not* be able to receive them. There were no visible bites on his brand-new skin, but assuming he was in the clear was a deadly gamble.

Our pediatrician returned with the academy's go-ahead. As far as they knew, Ben was the youngest person *ever* to get rabies shots. For the next four weeks, I took him to the hospital every Tuesday to receive two injections in his thighs. An elderly woman in the elevator saw the Band-Aids one day and cooed in his face. "Poor wittle baby! Is he sick? Why did this sweet wittle guy get shots in his wegs?

"Rabies," I said.

She got off on the next floor.

Though traumatic, Ben's experience is hardly unique. According to the Centers for Disease Control and Prevention, most Americans who contract rabies do so from bats, and the encounters often happen in their homes, sometimes in their sleep. About 70 percent of the 89 reported cases in the US between 1960 and 2018 were from bat exposures. However, it's important to note that less than 1 percent of bats will contract the disease. Two late 2020 deaths occurred because individuals didn't know they'd been bitten; a third victim was reportedly afraid of vaccines and refused the lifesaving, post-exposure prophylaxis despite the bat testing positive for rabies. Local health departments advise that a bat discovered in a bedroom should be contained and given immediately to health officials, who will euthanize and test it. Per the National Park Service, around 60,000 people receive the vaccine annually in the United States due to a potential rabies exposure.

Dr. Sheldon Owen of the West Virginia University Extension studies bats and educates the public about this unique group of mammals. He says West Virginia's heavy forests, thick canopies, caves, and clear-cut spaces are prime bat habitat. Some species migrate, while others move to winter hibernacula in caves, many of which are found in the eastern part of the state in counties like Randolph and Pendleton.

Around 25 percent of the mammal species on the planet are bats. They live on every continent except Antarctica. The smallest bat weighs two grams; the largest—the fruit-eating giant golden-crowned flying fox—has a wingspan of over five feet. Various species eat fruit, frogs, rats, and insects, among other things, but West Virginia species are all insectivores. Bats also spread seeds and pollinate, as in the case of the tequila agave plant, which is pollinated by the lesser long-nosed bat, a species that has recently come back from the brink of extinction. (I'll drink to that.) Most importantly, bats keep flying insects like mosquitos under control. That last point is important to remember when you've got a wayward bat in your house and you're ready to whack it with a broom. Bats *really* excel at insect control, so if you free that critter (and if it is safe to do so), it will go on to eat 6,000 to 8,000 insects *that night*. A colony of 100-some bats will devastate the mosquito population in your backyard, cutting your risk for dangers like West Nile, encephalitis, and Zika, as well as those welts that keep you up all night scratching your right ankle with your left toenail.

"We're talking metric tons of insects off the landscape each night," Owen said. The benefits go beyond our physical health. More bats mean fewer insects; fewer insects mean less pesticide and, ultimately, cheaper produce for the consumer. Without bats, you'd be standing in line at the produce market, legs smeared with calamine lotion, paying $8.50 for a Roundup-flavored cucumber.

Five of our twelve West Virginia species are threatened or endangered. Problems include habitat loss or changes, like deforestation. In addition, many cave-dwelling species are succumbing to White-nose

Syndrome. The fungus was discovered in 2006 in a New York cave. It easily spreads among hibernating colonies and is usually fatal. Studies have shown the disease can wipe out 90% of a site's population in fewer than five years.

According to Owen, "Our [endangered] Indiana bats hibernate in about seven caves across the United States. Seven caves, all of the population. So if we start losing even one of those caves, it's a significant impact on the bat population." It doesn't help that bats are slow reproducers and have one pup per year.

Though bats face numerous threats, we still feel threatened by them. The human fear response keeps us alive; it kept us from engaging with potentially harmful animals and situations. But our fear of bats is fed by misunderstanding. The bat is elusive and the folklore rich. There's a lot of false information floating around. For example, bats aren't rodents, they aren't blind, and they don't get caught in your hair. Owen said it's possible that an exhausted or baby bat *might* make contact with a person, but their echolocation usually keeps them well out of our way, as anyone who has ever tried to catch a bat discovers. They can see, but they rely on this technique to navigate and hunt, emitting sound waves and interpreting the signal as it bounces back, as dolphins do. It allows them to weave through heavy cover, amidst branches and around wires with ease. Most echolocation is well above our hearing range. But though it's high frequency, it's not a quiet sound at all.

"If we could hear it, it would probably deafen us," Owen said. "It's around 100 to 110 decibels. We're talking about a jackhammer."

Irrational or not, fear of bats is probably related to the human startle response more than anything. Our homes are supposed to be a sanctuary of safety. When a bat stumbles in, it brings with it all the ingredients for a panic attack: black wings, chaotic flight, a set of sharp teeth, and the remote but real possibility that it's carrying a deadly disease. I can't blame Shawn for his fear.

If bats are the stuff of nightmares, then my husband is not the first to have dreamed these creature dreams. The bat makes for an easy villain—his nature itself is suspect. He rises in the dark, feeds quietly, and indulges heartily. He's always out of reach, high enough in the air to be seen but never caught. We know now they are beneficial species, important for insect control and pollination, but how did the bat appear to generations past, centuries ago? With a ferocious snarl and an other-worldly chirp, bats were a confusing bundle of mistrust and dread. No wonder they figure so prominently in our collective stories.

Bats often represent the dark side. Mayan mythology associates the bat-god Camazotz with night, sacrifice, and death. In northern Scotland they were once thought to carry messages between witches and the devil, and according to some North American tribal folklore, they were viewed as tricksters or traitors, rejected by both birds and mammals. Rejection, it seems, is the bat's cross to bear, with a few exceptions. The Chinese consider the bat lucky, as do some northwestern Native American tribes. But mostly, they've been condemned. No wonder bats found themselves mixed up with the ultimate incarnation of evil, Count Dracula.

The notion of bloodsucking demons goes back to ancient times. Many cultures have a vampiric character in their mythologic repertoire, most often associated with the devil. In the Greek tradition, the *lamiai* seduced young men and fed on their blood. The Persians depicted blood-drinkers on their pottery, and in Old Norse the *draugr* was an undead devourer of flesh. However, it wasn't until the eighteenth century that the notion of vampires became a literary inspiration. While not the first to introduce vampire fiction, the Irish author Bram Stoker is certainly the most credited, and his Gothic horror novel *Dracula* became the template for modern vampiric lore. Count Dracula, unlike previous sanguineous incarnations, wasn't a bloated, bloodthirsty corpse. Possessing impeccable manners and tremendous wealth, he also commanded considerable strength, along with the ability to transform into fog, a wolf, and the most remembered iteration, a bat.

In the last few decades, a newer, sexier vampire culture has emerged in America. Books and television shows have recast the vampire as a suave, animalistic heartthrob, and audiences respond. The vampires of the twenty-first century still share a fair amount in common with Count Dracula; they're wealthy, well-dressed, and they hide from the sun. But they've divorced themselves from the bat, dropped the ability to transform into their winged doppelgängers. Bats no longer have a role; they've gotten the pink slip from the studios. Perhaps they're too simple and chaotic a creature to make a strong character element.

Perhaps the bat is too scary and hangs out in unseemly places; vampires nowadays sparkle and drink wine and drive Audis. The frenetic bat element is gone and, not-so-coincidentally, so is the element of pure vampiric evil. Most of today's vampires are decent and ethical, in fact they're usually the protagonists, which makes bats wrong for the part.

In reality, vampire bats reside only in Central and South America. They target goats and cattle, using their fangs to open a wound and lap up the blood rather than sucking it. Anticoagulants in their saliva keep the blood flowing, and scientists have recently been exploring possible uses for this property in blood clot and stroke patients. The vampire bat suffers from a bad reputation, and yet the statistics will confirm that, while they don't regularly attack humans, it's not unheard of. Attacks on humans have been triggered by the loss of their rainforest habitat.

They're hungry.

No one personifies the gray area inhabited by the bat better than the Dark Knight himself, Batman. I love Batman. He's everywhere: on my sons' pajamas, on *my* pajamas, and even on my neighbor's Toyota—the license plate reads "batmobl."

Apparently, everyone else loves Batman, too. He first appeared in DC Comics in 1939, one year after Superman's debut, but he was nothing like the Man of Steel. Superman—the ultimate incarnation of morality, standing tall, festooned in bright, honest red—did his superhero-ing in broad daylight. In Batman, creators were looking for an antihero, a vigilante. Batman was Superman's antithesis. Dark and morally ambiguous, he fought crime in the shadows, and he was a dark, obsessive loner, not quite a good guy. Unlike Superman, with his chiseled jaw and perfectly coiffed hair, Batman wore a cowl that obscured his face, and his sense of humor was decidedly lacking. The early Batman employed torture and showed little remorse over the killing of villains.

Like me, America loves Batman, with the possible exception of George Clooney's *Batman & Robin*. (It was the least successful of the films. And his bat-suit was the only one to feature nipples.) All told, the movie franchise is the ninth highest grossing film series of all time, earning almost seven billion and more than twice what the Superman movies have earned. Women, in particular, seem to swoon—it's the bad-boy image. Though dangerous and moody, he's ultimately a good guy under a layer of emotional turmoil. Superman is uncomplicated. He's 100 percent good. Batman is flawed, damaged. A real fixer-upper.

Bats are fixer-uppers, too. Their image needs a lot of work. The Endangered Species Act has benefited many species, but it's easy to work with a specimen like a bald eagle, the Superman of birds. Bald eagles don't drink blood, they don't spread disease, and they don't invade bedrooms. They have a strong jaw and a broad chest. Bats have a defensive attitude and smashed face. It's hard to love them. Bat conservationists like Dr. Owen have their work cut out for them, because the negativity toward bats goes back so far in our history. With a few cultural exceptions, we don't like them. We put their images up at Halloween along with bloody-faced ghouls. They're in every episode of Scooby-Doo, and they always signal the presence of fiends like the wolfman, aka Big Bob Oakley, the cantankerous groundskeeper, who's trying to throw the gang off the scent and keep the treasure for himself.

In real life, bats are in trouble. Even as conservationists work to change the bat's image, White-nose Syndrome spreads and wipes out colonies. That solution is up to science, while the job of the homeowner is to fight the demons—not those that fly, but those rampant fears that command us to grab a racket and swing. We can deal with bats, be vigilant but not foolhardy, because the bat is wild and he's afraid. He's not a bad guy. If we respect him, we can send him back outside to do his job in the hopes that his species will thrive.

It's a gray area, the bat world. To be sure, only human definitions can determine whether the bat is friend or foe. Nature doesn't care how we label its multitudes; it merely continues. Our categories are ours alone, and the bat has no solid category, nowhere he fits; rather, his label depends on whether he's flying out of doors or in. Is he helping the humans or terrorizing them? Even my husband, as he watches the sun go down, will remark that the bats are welcome to our mosquitos, but when they cross the boundary into our home, they become monsters. His mind is made up, and like the bat, he just can't help it.

Shawn and I still live in our old house. And as our years here have accumulated, so too have the number of little brown visitors. One January night, when Ben was two, Shawn helped me fold socks on the floor in the bedroom, and I found myself considering his trauma. Was he still frightened? I balled up a black toddler sock, hurled it at his face, and yelled, "Bat!" He shrieked and threw himself into the closet door, bashing his head against it in a desperate attempt to dodge the incoming threat. I collapsed in laughter, and he vowed never to help with laundry again. I apologized to him.

He told me to go fuck myself.

Nevertheless, in the last decade, we've both worked on our courage, and Shawn has actually gotten further than I have. Don't get me wrong: whenever a bat appears, we launch into a choreographed routine in which I scream and Shawn hides. More than once I've found him flat on the floor with a tennis racket over his face, hatching a plan to release venomous snakes into the roof so the problem "takes care of itself naturally." When I ask him how he's going to accomplish that, he tells me he's still working out the finer details.

But when one showed up in the living room the other night, we knew we had to deal with the intruder on our own. We were too embarrassed to call my dad. It would have been cruel to drag a seventy-three-year-old out of bed at midnight. Besides, we're middle-aged, and it was time to find our courage. We huddled together under the kitchen table, trying to pump each other up. Shawn had no plan other than to march in and wave a broom around, but this was a big step for him.

We dropped to our hands and knees and split up. I crawled into the foyer and peered into the living room, where the beast swooped in large, frenetic circles, and it was a whopper. I'm no expert, but I'd estimate a forty-two-inch wingspan. Our obese cat, Fur Pig, sat in the middle of the room and watched with bloated disinterest.

Shawn approached from the opposite direction. He lurked in the doorway, watching it flutter. When it came near, he sprang into the center of the room with surprising fortitude. Recalling his years of martial arts training, he assumed a ninja stance and swung the broom like a bō staff. But he didn't hit the bat; he hit the ceiling fan. The blades spun wildly, and the pull chain whipped around the motor as the entire contraption rocked back and forth.

Meanwhile, I still couldn't see from the nighttime ointment in my eyes, but I grabbed a hat and the first long object I could find in the broom closet and crawled into the living room. I figured if I could study the bat's flight pattern, maybe I could swat it at just the right moment and knock it to the floor. Then we could toss it outside in a towel.

The bat made several passes around me, and I tucked myself into the space beneath Shawn's desk. Each time it flew over, my bladder threatened to wave the white flag and saturate the rug. But then I remembered my kids, sleeping peacefully upstairs, and I knew I had to be brave. Holding my breath, I clutched my weapon and rose to my feet, still hunched low, but ready to swing. The bat seemed to know the fight was on and came at me. I roared and lashed the air above my head with my weapon. Panic would not rule the day. My adrenal glands came to life and courage washed through my veins—I could feel it. I wasn't scared any longer. I had the strength of a she-bear and the determination of a Viking, and this bat was leaving. The warrior was in total control.

Then something touched my ear. That was all it took. I screamed and threw myself on the floor, dropping my club to the wayside, only to realize that, in my blindness, I'd been brandishing a lime green pool noodle. The limp end had drooped down and brushed the side of my head, and I'd mistaken its Styrofoam caress for bat teeth. My courage evaporated and I belly-crawled back under Shawn's desk. Each time the black figure made a pass, I swatted at it from seven feet below with my flaccid flotation device.

In the other room, Shawn propped the front door open for an escape route. The terrified bat, of course, had no idea where it was supposed to go. So, to help its chances, Shawn opened the back door, too. Unfortunately for my husband, the habits of long-married people aren't likely to change just because a crisis is hanging on the crown molding. I had an opinion on the opening of doors and, as Shawn will tell you, I rarely keep my opinions to myself. From under the furniture, I disagreed with his course of action and emerged to close the back door.

He opened it. I closed it again.

"Why do you keep closing the back door?" he asked.

"Why are you opening two at the same time?" I countered.

"To increase the chances of getting it out," he said.

"That's a terrible idea," I said.

"Why?" he asked.

"You open *one* door and watch carefully so you can confirm that it leaves," I said. "Otherwise, you have no idea if it left or if it's just gone to sleep somewhere."

He said nothing.

"I'm right about this," I said. I say that a lot.

A strange look crossed his face. "Are you wearing a toboggan?" he asked.

"Yeah."

We both stared at each other for a moment, and then returned to the living room. Nothing moved. We'd lost track of the invader during our discussion. Shawn held his broom. I pulled my hat down over my eyebrows.

I hate it when they disappear. It means they've found a hiding place and gone to sleep. There's nothing more you can do, then, but go to bed and hope the animal isn't in your closet.

Knowing there's a bat in your house but not knowing where it lurks or when it will pop out is a special kind of hell. You're on edge the entire day. Any movement triggers panic. One minute you're making a turkey sandwich, and the next, a stray floater in your eye sends you headlong into the potato bin. You find yourself walking around with a ski mask and a wooden ladle, just in case.

The next morning, we found out that a rabid bat had been caught in the nearby neighborhood of Woodsdale. The health department advised everyone to be on alert and to dispatch any intruders and have them tested for rabies. This made our task even more unpleasant. Not only was the bat sleeping on some curtain or coat or hand towel, but there was a rabies concern. And there was an ugly task ahead of us.

The boys were eager to participate in the hunt; they didn't know it was going to end badly. They spent the day assembling an arsenal of Nerf guns, fishing nets, and ski gear, all part of what they assumed would be a stun-and-release operation. They devised their attack and ran practice drills. Everyone was on edge. The sun went down at 8:30, but the bat didn't appear. At nine, the house was still. We began searching rooms, expecting to see it circling, but found nothing. At 9:55, we told the kids the bat must have flown out one of the doors the night before when we were having our "discussion." They looked disappointed and shuffled off into their respective bedrooms, closing their doors behind them. Shawn went to his computer; I washed my face for bed.

At 10:04, I rounded a corner in the foyer and there it was. It had grown by at least 50 percent overnight. I didn't need to call the team; at the sound of my scream, their doors opened, and they stormed out of their rooms, locked, loaded, and terrified. A hail of foam bullets rained down.

In the end, of course, nobody came within five feet of the bat with their mock weaponry. They shot my china cabinet. They shot my curtains. Somebody took out an Ecuadorian wall hanging and somebody else grazed the dog's ear. Eventually, they switched to a fishing net, which turned out to be a more effective tool than the Zombie Strike Blaster. We found the bat hanging on the curtain in my office. Shawn, in an uncharacteristic act of fortitude, stepped into the room and dealt the final blow with the net.

The boys, who'd been caught up in the excitement of a mission they thought would end with the bat's freedom and salvation—rough though the process might be—saw it die, and they fell apart. Their tears flowed for the tiny creature, an accidental intruder who took an unfortunate wrong turn and paid the ultimate price.

The rabies test came back negative.

I suspect I'm not alone, crouching there in my snowsuit with my pool noodle. These critters intimidate. But despite the trauma of an invasion, I ask for tolerance on their behalf. More than anything, bats need a change of the human heart. It's not as simple as writing a check at a charity event. We need to collectively thaw out, to free them from our demonology and our paranoia. Bats need our support, our respect, and they need us to spread the word—the truth. They need understanding. We want our mosquitos eaten, our trees pollinated. So let us remember that the little black terror hanging on the curtains is probably a baby, confused and lost beyond a hope. Let us choose to appreciate the flappy bat with his leathery wings and defiant hiss, because he's here to do his job, and we need him so much more than he needs us. It's time to embrace our inner girly-shrieks. Let's admit why we're *really* buying that bass net and sleeping in the Honda. Own your terror,

West Virginia. It's okay to dive under furniture. It's okay to don hockey masks and laundry baskets and belly-crawl across the floor. And yes, it's okay to scream.

# Behold, the Caddisfly

K athy Stout was a respiratory therapist by day, and in her spare time, she made jewelry. While most artists and craftsmen labor over every detail, her role in the creative process didn't come until the end. She attached chain and wire, but caddisflies did most of the work.

Like many other aquatic macroinvertebrates, caddisflies spend their larval stages in streams, and when it's time to pupate, they build protective cases out of the materials around them. Some caddisfly species use pebbles to create cases, some use leaves, and others use tiny sticks. When they emerge as new adults, they rise to the surface, molt, and fly away. The adults live just long enough to mate and for the female to lay her eggs on vegetation above the surface of the water.

The presence or lack of macroinvertebrates in a stream is a good indicator of water quality. A search under rocks reveals a cast of characters that corresponds to dissolved oxygen levels, pH, and temperature. They can also signal pollution. Midge larvae and aquatic worms can tolerate a fair amount of pollution; scuds, dragonflies, and damselflies are far more sensitive. The least tolerant insects are the mayflies, stoneflies, and caddisflies. Finding them is a good sign.

Kathy's husband was a West Virginia stream ecologist. Aquatic biology was a way of life, and she began to wonder what would happen if the caddisflies were given gemstones rather than river pebbles to build their cases. Curiosity led Kathy to streams with good water quality in search of larval caddisflies. She brought them home, gave them colorful substrates, and discovered that the insects didn't give a hoot what hue their stones were. By the time I came home from my freshman year of college looking for work, she had built a lab in her garage.

I tended to the caddisflies that summer. They lived in a dozen large plastic tubs in the lab. Each tub was filled with water, littered with leaves—the insects' primary food source—and a substrate consisting of the chosen stone. There was the malachite tub, the pyrite tub, the opal tub. She offered them abalone, sodalite, unakite. In one tub, she offered them regular stream pebbles. In another, she kept the species that made their cases out of sticks for a more natural alternative. Bubbling air stones oxygenated the water. In later years, Kathy created a far more sophisticated system in the lab that simulated the movement of a stream, but she was only a few years into the project when I met her.

The difficulty lay in keeping the water in the plastic bins cool. West Virginia mountain streams are chilly—cold water means more oxygen—and the summer temperatures (in a garage, no less) were a constant threat to the insects' survival. Plus, the lack of current to carry away their waste meant that somebody had to get rid of it for them.

That somebody was me. On resumes I would later create, my title was "Benthic Macroinvertebrate Laboratory Technician." In reality, I was the bug shit cleaner.

Each morning, I hauled the tubs to the sink, drained the old, dirty water, and refilled them. I had to be careful not to let any of the larvae or stones go down the drain, and I had a pretty good success rate. Sometimes I'd find a dead caddisfly, but overall, they kept busy munching leaves and crawling around with their abdomens tucked into their cases, hermit crab style. At the end of the season, when they emerged as adults, Kathy would open the laboratory windows and the caddisflies would fly away to begin their life cycles anew. Each year, she traveled to healthy streams to recruit more larvae for the program.

Not all streams in West Virginia are as clear and clean as they appear, though, especially in the southern coalfields where surface mountaintop removal mining is prevalent. Whereas traditional mining is done underground, mountaintop removal is easier, cheaper, and safer. It's a multistep process: 1. Remove the "overburden." This is the forested top of the mountain that the coal companies blast off with dynamite. 2. Harvest the coal with bulldozers. 3. Dump the leftovers into the valley beside the mountain. Six hundred vertical feet of rock and ash may pile up in the hollow, and anything that lived, tunneled, or flowed there is entombed. Forever.

Kathy's husband, Dr. Ben Stout, became an expert on the deleterious effects of mountaintop removal. Over the years, he testified in many court cases, even taking one judge out into a frozen stream to witness

Deep & Wild

the devastation the mining had wrought. The judge wore rubber boots, and he ultimately ruled against the coal company in question.

In the 2008 documentary *Burning the Future: Coal in America*, director David Novack followed Ben to various mining sites. In a quiet scene, Dr. Stout stands on the edge of an irregular tract, terraced on one side and sloping down to a highwall. Rough grass covers the bare land like a five o'clock shadow. He looks grim.

"Even under perfect conditions, it would take thousands of years for that to return back to the ancestral forest, but I doubt that will ever happen," he says. "A forest will grow back on that valley fill eventually, but it'll never be anything like the original forest that was there."

The central Appalachian hardwood forest is the second-most diverse ecosystem on earth, after the Amazon rainforest. An enormous variety of hardwood trees grow there; it contains more species of trees, birds, and amphibians than almost any other ecological community.

Per 1977's Surface Mining Control and Reclamation Act, coal companies must reclaim the land and repair the damage they've caused after mining is complete. But with the decline of coal, many can't afford to do so, and even when they can, the act does not require them to reforest the land. They often plant inexpensive, non-native grasses that take over and make it harder for the original forest to grow and the wildlife it supports to return. Moreover, like the Amazon rainforest, the Appalachian forest acts as a carbon sink, capturing carbon dioxide that would otherwise go into the atmosphere and contribute to climate change. Deforestation, on the other hand, could turn a helpful carbon sink into a harmful carbon source by 2025.

None of this is new. Coal companies have been whacking off the tops of West Virginia mountains for decades. And while production has increased by over 50% since the 1980s, employment has dropped by 65%. The jobs that were done, underground, by hundreds of miners can be done now with dynamite and a few bulldozers. Over 500 mountains have been destroyed in Central and Southern Appalachia; Google Earth shows a long swath of tan pockmarks on the folded, emerald skin of southwestern West Virginia. More than 2,000 miles of headwater streams have been buried by fill. Heavy metals including lead, arsenic, and mercury may leach into the groundwater and turn southern West Virginians' well water yellow, brown, and black. Life in many streams is nonexistent, as are the streams themselves, buried under the broken bodies of the mountains they sculpted. I've seen the grisly orange scars from the window of a Boeing 737, where the soft velvet of deciduous forest has been ripped from the rock beneath. It looks like a boneyard.

After it's mined, coal is washed at a prep plant and the slurry deposited in a retention pond. Slurry ponds are susceptible to failure, and when they fail, the resulting flood can destroy a stream . . . or a community. On February 26, 1972, in one of West Virginia's most notorious and tragic disasters, three slurry pond impoundment dams managed by the Pittston Coal Company failed. A wall of water thirty feet high rushed down the Buffalo Creek hollow in Logan County and swept 16 towns away with 132 million gallons of black wastewater. The flood killed 125 people and destroyed the homes of 4,000 more. Pittston claimed the accident was an act of God. The state sued the company for $100 million in damages, and the case languished in the courts for years. Days before he left office, Governor Arch Moore accepted a $1 million settlement, though additional cleanup cost another $9 million. Pittston also settled with the families, each of whom received around $13,000, after legal fees.

Every West Virginian knows Buffalo Creek. We learn about it in elementary school—a tragedy that has become a bitter touchstone. The mention of the disaster grinds conversation to a halt. We stop, nod, and mumble a somber acknowledgment. *Yeah, that was awful.* Because there's little else to say under the weight of its horror. And though the state has seen its share of disasters wrought by the hands of both man and nature, the flood that roared through that hollow took not only lives and property, but it also swept away our peace of mind. The water drowned our people, their families, their histories. A *what if* turned into an *if only*—if only they'd been out of the house. If only they'd had some warning. If only the dam had held.

But dam failures happen. A similar disaster struck in 2000 in Martin County, Kentucky, just across the Ohio River, when the bottom of a Massey Energy slurry pond gave way and flooded a mine beneath. The spill, which was thirty times larger than the Exxon Valdez oil spill,

Deep & Wild

poured out of mine openings and into the watershed. In 2008, a coal ash pond gave way in Tennessee, releasing 1.1 billion gallons of slurry that covered 300 acres of land. Over 30 people on the cleanup crew died of cancer within a decade.

The DNR stocks Buffalo Creek with trout now, and fishermen stand in the pools, fly poles in hand, hoping the rainbows will rise to their lures. It's taken fifty years, considerable cleanup, and remediation to make the stream habitable for trout again, but other creeks and hollows may never fully recover. While I was tending to the caddisflies in the late nineties, though, only half that time had passed, and at nineteen, I knew next to nothing about mountaintop removal.

Despite my employers' growing connection to the issue, most of the lab chores were tedious, but I got to know my tiny charges as they grew over the summer. Some caddisfly groups were rowdier than others, throwing subaquatic soirées under the leaf litter, while other tubs were full of layabouts and deadbeats who crawled lazily through their larvalhoods. All the caddisflies instinctively built their cases, but some excelled. The abalone group was always productive and focused. The sodalite group, on the other hand, seemed a little too chill, like the stoner kids who sit in the back of the class and ask distracting existential questions like, "Do birds know they're birds?" and "What if we could hear cheese?" Still, every surviving larva built a beautiful case, and as the summer progressed, I grew attached. When they died prematurely, I washed their tiny bodies down the drain. It would have been nice to return them to their native streams, even in death.

I had duties outside the lab, too. Kathy had the artistic vision and talent, so she created each piece of jewelry. Before the cases could be strung on a chain and accented with beads or gems, though, they had to be reinforced. Caddisflies make a glue-like silk that holds their cases together, and it works well for their purposes. But for daily use in human life—dangling from a neck or earlobe—they needed to be reinforced with epoxy we mixed. The very scientific recipe was a whole paper plate of ingredient number one plus one-half a paper plate of ingredient number two. We stirred the concoction with a toothpick, swirling in circles until the goo came together. And you'd think that rudimentary formula would be easy to follow, but it wasn't.

Kathy mixed the glue for me each day, but by July, she decided I could handle the task on my own. I'd kept her caddisflies alive. I'd looked after her sweet boys several times. And really, anyone could mix glue.

Except me. Despite my young life's successes—an improbable A in Calculus, a year in school on my own, and the newfound skill to hand-filter dung out of a Walmart Rubbermaid bin—I couldn't whip up a usable epoxy. Moreover, we couldn't know if the mix was a success or a failure until it was applied and the caddisfly cases had dried. A successful glue produced a hard, sturdy case, but if it crumbled under pressure, the epoxy had been mixed improperly. It was a mind game, and the glue thwarted anyone who sought to unlock the deep magic of craft store adhesives.

Kathy was kind and patient, and she never held it against me when I destroyed the valuable inventory, which I did, often. Not only was I a literal homewrecker, but I was also the kind of monster who took out entire neighborhoods. I trashed them in batches: fifteen abalone on a Tuesday, nineteen jasper on a Thursday, and on one devastating July afternoon, two dozen malachite cases. Kathy called me at home with a question, and in passing, I asked how they'd turned out. She paused, and I knew it was bad.

"Well," she started. "The epoxy didn't hold. But don't worry about it. I've ruined plenty." At the time, malachite was the most expensive stone she used. I hung up the phone and cried for what I'd done, to her and to the caddisflies, who had spent their lives constructing their cases, their magnum opera. And then I showed up.

You may remember the story of a painting by Spanish painter Elías García Martínez called *Ecce Homo* ("Behold the Man"). It's a famous fresco of Jesus, crowned with thorns, that hangs in a church in Borja, Spain. In 2012, it needed a facelift and fell into the hands of an elderly, untrained parishioner who did her best to restore it. What resulted was a gruesome—and, admittedly, hilarious—figure so altered and simian it was mockingly dubbed "*Ecce Mono.*" ("Behold the monkey.") Ironically, the church and town now see almost quadruple the number of tourists, most of whom come to view the painting, which is also referred to as "Potato Jesus."

When the story broke, I laughed at the botched restoration attempt. But I'm equally guilty, because for three months during the summer of 1998, I potato-Jesused the hell out of those poor caddisflies' great work. After the malachite massacre, I left the glue mixology to the experts. Careless hands shouldn't tinker with a masterpiece.

I went back to the lab and continued changing the water as July melted into a sweltering August. The caddisflies snuggled into their cases and began the most important work of their brief lives. Time grew short for me, too—college was starting again, and my departure felt anticlimactic. After a summer of bug-sitting, I would miss the hatch and their return to the wild.

🐜

Studies have established the link between mountaintop removal sites and lung cancer. Children born near a mountaintop removal site are 41% more likely to be born with birth defects than those who aren't. Compared to the whole of Appalachia, cancer rates are far higher in mountaintop mining communities. Some groups have cast doubt on the link, however, including a law firm representing several coal companies and the National Mining Association. The firm argued, in writing, that "the study failed to account for consanquinity [sic], one of the most prominent sources of birth defects." For the record, consanguinity (with a $g$) refers to shared ancestry. Inbreeding.

The reference would have come as no surprise to any West Virginian. Our stereotypes are an easy reach for anyone looking to discredit us, and blaming us for our own tragedies is a long-standing tradition. *Well, of course West Virginians die in slurry floods . . . they're obsessed with fossil fuels and they marry their cousins.* And while we've come to expect aspersions, our detractors hurl them at the cruelest moments, like when we're laying family members to rest in the same soil that poisoned them.

The law firm retracted their statement and apologized, specifying the message was taken out of context. Not that it mattered, because floods will continue as the confluence of deforestation and climate change—the effects of which often include torrential storms in Appalachia—magnifies the risk. It's unclear if federal help will arrive—the

Behold, the Caddisfly

Biden administration, which vowed to focus on environmental justice and complete an Obama-era review of the research on mining health risks, has yet to move on the issue of mountaintop removal and the health of nearby communities.

It's hard to know what will become of our mountains, and West Virginians themselves are divided on the issue. Some locals hang signs on their porches when protesters are in town. *Tree huggers suck. Go home. Git a job. Take a bath.* After all, coal's paychecks have paid for many generations' homes and schooling. Understandably, loyalties often lie with whoever puts food on the table. Moreover, some voices in the conversation speak with comforting authority. In *Burning the Future*, the documentary crew interviews a marketing manager at a West Virginia Caterpillar dealer who describes his company's role in the mountaintop removal process.

"As they run the dozers to put the land back, it's almost an artistic activity to watch the way they sculpt the mountains in really a great manner," he says. His dialogue overlays a clip of a bulldozer shoving blackened overburden off the edge of an ashy, orange cliff. Next comes a pro-surface-mining advertisement. The camera pans over a flattened, grassy plateau, dotted with the occasional invasive autumn olive bush. The land is green but devoid of forest. A friendly baritone voice oozes confidence all over the TV screen.

"Over time," the voice assures us, "Mother Nature lends a helping hand, and soon it's hard to tell what was mined and what was not. Mountaintop mining and beautiful, rugged mountains: We *can* have both. That's the way it ought to be."

🍂

Ben Stout continued to fight for water quality and the health of affected West Virginians. In a terrible loss to the state, he died of cancer in 2018, leaving behind his sons and a legacy of environmental activism in a place where his voice was so desperately needed. And while mountaintops in southern West Virginia continue to fall, the movement he helped shape still trudges forward, in sorrow and hope.

But my summer with the caddisflies stayed with me. After all my water changes, the hauling of tubs, and the quiet work the animals had done, they emerged from their bejeweled cases and rose from the water for the first time. Sometimes, they sat on Kathy's finger, a brief moment of connection in the final weeks of their lives, during which they would mate, lay eggs, and fade away into the hollows and streams.

I'd already gone back to college. I missed the completion of their tiny existence, never got to see them born into their final forms. Kathy told me about the moment she opened the lab windows, though. With their sparkling cases forgotten, the new adults found their footing as warm air flooded the room. Instinct took over, and in a rising swell, off they went into the world. She said it was beautiful—hundreds of amber wings unfurled and disappeared into the sky.

# Snagging a Spot for Stumpy

**W**e called the giant silver maple in my backyard "Stumpy." It wasn't alone out there—it stood among oak, ash, gum, walnut, poplar, sycamore, buckeye, elm, locust, dogwood, crab, magnolia, redbud, hemlock, pine, spruce, and cedar, all in little more than an acre. (We really like trees in my family.) The old maple grew on the west side of the yard, where it blocked the late afternoon heat and sheltered us from storm winds. The lightest breeze flipped its soft leaves and rolled sterling waves over the canopy. In the spring, seedpods called samaras spun like tiny helicopters; in early fall, pale golden leaves whispered their way down to the drying grass.

Silver maples often suffer storm damage, as ours did during the derecho of June 29, 2012. A fast-moving storm characterized by intense winds, the meteorological monster was born in a thunderstorm cell in Iowa and grew into one of the deadliest and costliest derechos in US history. Over the course of 12 hours, it blew across Central Appalachia with winds peaking at 91 miles per hour, mowing down trees, roofs, and powerlines in its 700-mile path until it petered out over the Atlantic Ocean. Appalachian Power had never seen damage like it. Twenty-two people died, many from falling trees. Half of West Virginia sat in the dark, and some people in the mountains continued to limp along without power for more than 2 weeks. For some, a record-breaking heat wave turned the extended outage deadly.

Many people in Wheeling sustained some sort of damage during that event—a barn, a car, a roof. We tried to remember our fortune as we sat in the sweltering, wet dark with two young children, watching our phone batteries plummet until YouTube finally faded to black and a mournful cry rose up from our sweaty souls. It was a rough couple of nights, but we were lucky.

None of our trees sustained any obvious damage, but the silver maple's limbs began to fall the year after the derecho. One landed on our lawn chairs just moments after the kids and I vacated them, and hefty branches dropped out of the canopy on calm, clear days. We called in an expert for an assessment, who saw signs of disease and suggested we top the tree in the hopes that it would encourage new growth, despite the poor prognosis. Topping is a practice that removes most of the upper bulk. It's a severe haircut that leaves little more than a torso with sawed-off limbs. To recover, the tree sends out new branches, but they're thin and flimsy, and it will never really recover from the buzz cut. Moreover, sawing off major limbs leaves open wounds that invite in disease and insects. Topping is a poor way to handle trees, especially silver maples, because it creates weak growth, damages the branching structure, and leaves the tree looking like a forty-foot hat rack. Nevertheless, we saw no other choices. Topping it was a safety measure and a last-ditch attempt to revive the being we had named Stumpy, though we knew it was unlikely to work.

Once the tree was topped, we watched it for a few years, waiting to see if new shoots would grow. Instead, nature sent in its own experts: fungi and woodpeckers. The former sprouted along the trunk; the latter—our resident, red-bellied woodpecker pair—inspected the tree and decided to call it home. They pecked, drilled, and bored, and their presence meant Stumpy housed a thriving insect community. Likewise, the fungi indicated predictable disease and decay.

It was over.

In forestry terms, Stumpy had become a *snag*. Snags are so common in the woods that we barely notice them, but in a suburban yard, it was a stark reminder of death amidst summer's vibrancy. And despite its hulking and somewhat creepy presence, time and money got away from us, so Stumpy stood in place.

I was embarrassed. After all, what respectable suburbanite keeps a dead tree around? Not only might it fall and crush you, but it also looks hideous and unkempt with its trunk pockmarked with mushrooms and two fat limbs severed just above the crotch. Visitors to the yard started commenting.

"Uh, that tree doesn't look so good."

"Hey, I think your tree might be dead."

"What's the deal with that . . . *thing* over there?"

Usually, I made up a story about how it was just a temporary situation and the snag was coming down next week. I do the same thing when the house is a mess and a visitor or service person drops by. *Oh, don't mind this mess. You caught me on laundry day. When you showed up I was totally about to put all this stuff away and definitely not sitting in my hamburger-print fleece pants watching Road Runner cartoons and questioning my life's choices.*

I hoped for the tree's theatrical demise, that it might fall on its own and save us the time and cost of removing it. But even in death, it remained sturdy. And without its silver-green sails to catch the wind, storms merely blew past it. No matter how stupid it looked, Stumpy was going nowhere.

There's something raw and aggressively uncaring about a snag. There it stands, bereft of life, but still far more useful than we will ever be, alive or dead. No matter how hard we try, we can only host one or two life forms at a time (for the really hardcore uteruses, maybe three), and we can't even do that without nausea, hemorrhoids, and sneeze-induced bladder leakage. Snags, on the other hand, are a community unto themselves, with the potential to support over a thousand wildlife species. Ours offered the red-bellied woodpeckers a place to feed and raise their young. In the spring, the pair excavated a nest cavity. When the chicks fledged at the end of May, we watched from our deck as they hopped about on Stumpy's stumpy arms. They took their first tentative test-flights, and we gasped at their tumbles and narrow escapes from the jaws of our German shepherd. (There's nothing quite so traumatic as gathering your kids for one of nature's miraculous events only to witness the family dog yak up Woody Woodpecker's partially digested foot in the day lilies.) As the morning wore on, the chicks got the hang of flying, and their father led them each on undulating practice runs through the trees. By that afternoon, the pecker parents had done their job and the family moved out, though they continued to reside in our little suburban forest and visit Stumpy at mealtimes. The next year, they excavated a new nest hole just below the previous year's.

After the woodpeckers left, other species moved in. Mammalian cavity nesters can include squirrels, opossums, weasels, raccoons, and, if the cavity is large enough, black bears. (I don't think West Virginia woodpeckers are creating the bear holes, but if so, the Department of Natural Resources should probably focus less on trout and more on gamma radiation.) Other birds, too, make good use of snag cavities, and more birds means fewer insects, fewer weeds, and better pollination. Additionally, species who don't live in the tree will still use the tree. Stumpy's upper branches serve as a perch and a launchpad for Cooper's, sharp-shinned, and red-tailed hawks.

Nocturnal creatures will occupy a hole, as well. Screech owls keep the rodent population down. One little brown bat consumes thousands of mosquitos each night. To that end, we hung a bat house on Stumpy's lower regions, roughly fifteen feet off the ground. The bats never took to it, but our favorite fox squirrel, Slappy, sat on it and nibbled his nuts each morning. Eventually, the tree's odd, limbless form became part of the landscape, as did the familiar creatures crawling over and through it.

There's something defiant about a snag, whether or not it intends to defy. Snags stand around. They lean. Eventually, they crash to the ground—not that they care. The snag is retired. It's done a lifetime of work, rising up through the canopy from sapling to spruce or oak or beech. It's grown branches, made seedlings of its own, housed birds, fed insects, and now the poor thing just wants to quietly rot away in peace. But we don't want that. We don't want to deal with a snag—what if it falls on us? On our house? On our new car? Sure, we love our trees, but once a tree dies, it moves from commodity to liability. Not to mention an eyesore on the manicured American lawn that may take up to a century to disappear.

When we, the short-lived humans die, not only do we break down quickly, but the other humans take great pains and bear phenomenal expense to make sure that our remains are disposed of before that process begins. We *could* hang around and make ourselves useful, as the snags do. We could host bacteria, insects, plant life. We could feed a pack of hungry street dogs or, if the rumors about nonchalant felines digesting their owners are true, the cat we leave behind. But nobody wants to see that. The woods may have no shame, but *we* do. Nobody wants Great-Aunt Millie propped up against the living room wall in a state of decomposing repose.

Except for a group of hearty souls at the University of Tennessee. The Anthropological Research Facility, aka the Body Farm, is an outdoor

Deep & Wild

decomposition laboratory where the dead do the only thing they can on their own: break down. Some bodies are left exposed, some are buried in shallow graves, some are submerged in water or mud. By studying the stages of human decay in various situations, forensic researchers, medical professionals, and law enforcement personnel can get a better picture of when a person died, how they died, and what might have done them in. Thirty-six years ago, when the facility opened, the public was horrified. But the farm's fame has grown with references on TV shows like *CSI: Crime Scene Investigation*, and it was the inspiration for Patricia Cornwall's novel, *The Body Farm*, so the citizens of Knoxville aren't quite so edgy about the important work being done there.

Nevertheless, body farms unsettle us on many levels—the smell, the indignity of death out in the open, and the idea that a loved one might be rotting in the Volunteer State sun. It's hard enough to accept the impossible notion that every one of us is going to die (quite frankly, I still think I might be the one who manages to escape that fate, I just haven't put enough effort into it, yet), and it's disturbing to think of anything happening to our body after we've vacated it. Death may be conditionally acceptable if we imagine ourselves well-dressed and going out in style. But to be dumped out on the lawn and left to whatever bugs and varmints sniff out our sloppy pile of guts? Holy shit. That would totally wipe out all those years we've devoted to creating an image. All those years of sucking in our stomachs for the camera, wasted.

But the snag embraces it. The snag, in a manner that I've merely imagined because humans anthropomorphize *everything* and can't just talk about death in plain language, knows its fate and leans into it, literally. It sheds its leaves, lies down on the forest floor—at which point it becomes a log—and gives itself over to the process of death, which in nature is not the opposite of life but merely a subset of it. Nature doesn't care who lives and dies—*we* do. We can't stand the inequity, the unfairness of it all, and whatever's dying in front of us is nature's most tragic victim. We watch shows with Sir David Attenborough and cringe when orcas snatch a baby seal off the beach. But in the next show, when the whalers load up their harpoon, we throw things at the television and mail fifty bucks off to Greenpeace to support the guys in the little rubber boat.

**Snagging a Spot for Stumpy**                                          **117**

Fortunately for our delicate human sensibilities, there are a lot of ways to dispose of ourselves that don't involve rotting on the forest floor or in an outdoor laboratory. But the two most common are no friend to the environment or the forests of Stumpies out there. American cemeteries take up a million acres of land and require water, gas-powered lawncare, and insecticide applications. Four million acres of forest go annually into the construction of wooden caskets and coffins; 800,000 gallons of formaldehyde go into the bodies they contain. Likewise, cremation, which seems like a more natural way to get rid of your useless, old corpse, isn't at all. The process produces 534 pounds of $CO_2$ per body. That's 360,000 metric tons per year, to say nothing of the toxic chemicals released into the atmosphere including but not limited to nitrogen oxides, sulfur dioxide, mercury, and volatile organic compounds like those notoriously pungent, postmortem beer farts.

Slowly, though, greener forms of burial are emerging. You can be cremated in a vat of water, through the process of alkaline hydrolysis, which reduces a body to the same pile of bones traditional cremation would. That's far friendlier to the planet, and now, even more interesting options have emerged. One funeral home in Seattle will compost you, which turns out to be a useful way to say goodbye.

Cheryl Strayed recalls in *Wild* that she swallowed one of her cremated mother's bones in a moment of grief. That's certainly an option, but it's a one-time deal. If you go the composting route, however, your family can enjoy Great-Aunt Millie-flavored cucumbers all summer long. And it's a little easier on the teeth.

You can also be buried in a tree pod, which is a fancy way of saying they stuff you into a big egg and a tree grows out of your head. (More or less.) The inventor of the tree pod envisions not cemeteries and marble headstones but a memorial forest, complete with woodpeckers. Alternatively—and this one is my favorite—someone has designed a mushroom burial suit. Instead of your finest farewell togs, you're buried in cotton clothing woven with mushroom spores, with or without a simple casket. And then, as with snags, the fungi supposedly go to work, reducing your body to enzymes. While some doubt the efficiency of the process, it's billed as a green alternative to the formaldehyde bath you'd get at the funeral home. Mycelium, the network of fungal threads beneath the

Deep & Wild

ground that gives rise to fruiting bodies like mushrooms is known for its ability to neutralize toxins like lead, mercury, and pesticides. Thanks to our cultural obsession with Roundup and the prevalence of mercury dental fillings, we've all got a cocktail of poison running through our veins, but the 'shrooms are on the job.

Likewise, the 'shrooms did their best to break Stumpy down. They climbed up the trunk and sprouted in grays, whites, and browns from the faded, chipping bark. Shelf fungi ooched in next to club fungi, and they worked in concert to soften the wood.

It might have been a decade before these processes weakened the snag enough to topple it, but there was no way to know when that day might come. I loved that Stumpy had fed and sheltered so many of our wildlife, but eventually, safety took precedence. After several years of faithful service to the backyard eco-community, it had to come down before it lost the ability to stand. We called the tree guys, who came out with their bucket truck and their chainsaws. They didn't have far to climb—Stumpy was only twenty-five feet tall. Nor was it a long job. With only two partially amputated limbs, it was a matter of sawing them off in thick sections until just the shaft of the tree remained. My sons settled into lawn chairs to watch. They'd always been the tree guys' biggest fans: as toddlers they watched the men grind stumps and feed logs into the gaping mouth of their wood chipper. Apparently, the kids weren't the only ones fascinated by the work, because passersby stopped to peer into the yard, hoping to catch the big moment.

"People stand around and watch when we're taking a tree down," one of them told me as another made the final cut at Stumpy's base, the one that would turn our snag into a log. "Everyone's waiting for the sky show."

When Stumpy hit the ground, I expected a crash, the kind of reverberating, multisyllable *crack-crack-slam* you hear when a tree falls in the woods. (Unless, of course, no one is around to hear it.) But without branches to snap and other trees to crush as collateral damage, what was left of the silver maple hit the grass with a hollow-sounding *thud*, bounced once, and settled immediately into the log life (#LogLife). The corroded stump, once exposed, revealed that Stumpy was as dead on the inside as it was on the outside. Within a month, fungi popped up from its flat expanse, and Ben and I took to dancing on it when we were feeling silly. We called it the Stump Dance.

Unlike snags, stumps make me uncomfortable. Like many Gen X children, I was mildly traumatized by Shel Silverstein's *The Giving Tree*, a seemingly sweet story about a tree that gives every part of her arboreal body to a little boy as he grows into a man. Piece by piece, he takes her entire being for himself—to impress a woman, to build his house and a boat, and then to sail away and leave her a sad, lonely stump. In the last pages, he returns, an old man in need of one final thing: a place to sit. And since she's a stump, she's got nothing else to do but hold up his elderly ass. And because she's female—Mother Nature herself, our endless source of life, fuel, and wealth—she happily does so. (Codependency always makes for an uplifting bedtime read.) I've grown to hate the book and the narcissistic boy-man and Shel Silverstein, too, for planting the idea that the maternal entities of the world need to give and give until they're naught but a rotting, mushroom-ridden log, and even then, they should be grateful they can offer some old white guy's butt a spot to plant its wrinkly cheeks. Silverstein once defended the book, saying it was simply about a relationship between a giver and a taker. Indeed, it is.

We never asked Stumpy for much, though. We gave it a place to grow, and it offered us shade and a few near-death experiences. We lived, and it lived, until we claimed the fading years of its afterlife. But the defiant stump didn't care what form it took any more than the snag or the tree had, so after the fungi did their work for a few more years, we ground it up until the last visible traces were gone, because it was difficult to mow around. It would have been better to leave it—as a snag, or a log, or a stump—but humans are indeed takers, whether out of greed or convenience. And so, the yard changed, again. Without Stumpy's shielding curtain, full sun hit the garden and the shade-loving perennials scorched in the heat. I planted bee balm and echinacea for the pollinators. Butterflies came, and hummingbirds. The woodpeckers pecked and fledged in the black walnut tree. Sharp-shinned hawks perched in the pin oak. Beneath the ground, the silver maple's ghostly roots decomposed and released their elemental ingredients back into the earth, and the soil where the tree stood darkened and smelled of peat and humus and worm poop.

Deep & Wild

# The Value of Wind

**M**y husband and I have a lot in common, but one thing we cannot agree on is the value of wind. Wind drives me nuts, but he loves windy days. He loves watching trees thrash and leaves fly by. He rejoices as a gust front blows through, and, in his heart, I believe the man prays for the occasional microburst. We had one, years ago, and he still talks about how a Mickey Mouse bucket in the backyard flew forty feet over top of the house and landed in the front yard. Limbs came down and transformers blew, but it was the bucket that really marked that day as a watershed weather event. The Bucket of 2012.

Shawn is especially fascinated by tornadoes. In West Virginia, we don't get a lot of them. It's true that nowhere on earth is tornado-free; one *could* touch down almost anywhere, and they've been recorded on every continent except Antarctica. They've touched down on the top of Pittsburgh's Mount Washington, the high hill that overlooks downtown Pittsburgh and the confluence of its three rivers. West Virginia's deadliest tornado outbreak occurred in 1944 when a series of twisters killed 103 people. According to the National Oceanic and Atmospheric Administration, West Virginia gets a yearly average of 2 (as opposed to Texas, which endures around 137). We can thank our mountains because the higher you rise, the cooler and more stable the air gets—poor conditions for storm generation. That said, a tornado can form anywhere, and global warming has brought with it more severe weather, here, including increased tornadic activity. Fortunately, when they do spawn, they usually drop down, mangle a toolshed, and then recede into the clouds. If you look at a map of local tornado paths in the last 65 years, most of them have been on the low-elevation West Virginia-Ohio border, with very few in the eastern mountainous region.

In the last decade and a half, the effects of climate change have revealed themselves in some very active tornado seasons in the United States. Places like Tuscaloosa, Alabama, and Joplin, Missouri, have seen devastating tornadoes, and Shawn can tell you all about each one. He can describe the conditions, recall the date. He can tell you where any given tornado landed on the Fujita scale. He can tell you about the Tri-State tornado that traveled over 219 miles in 1925 and the 1974 F5 in Xenia, Ohio, that killed 32 people and leveled half the town.

In the summer of 2009, a potentially tornadic storm formed to our west. We get tornado watches, but they rarely graduate into warnings. Shawn was on high alert, armed with the software that meteorologists and tornado chasers use. (He's given me lessons on how to read radar and spot the debris ball that indicates the exact location of the tornado itself, but it hasn't sunk in. All I see on the screen is a red blob next to a yellow blob in the center of some green blobs and *oh look there's a Weather Channel ad for 15 percent off all queen-sized duvet covers at Target.*)

As the storm approached, he watched the radar, the news, and the sky. There were no reports of an actual funnel cloud, but radar indicated rotation (and, when I checked, free shipping). The emergency broadcast system squealed, and for the first time in my life in the Mountain State, the television told me to gather my family and get underground.

"Okay, buddy," I said to three-year-old Andy. "Let's go into the back basement." The foundation had been dug into the sloping hillside, and it was the safest spot in the house. I wasn't truly frightened, because severe storms usually fall apart when they cross the Ohio River and drop down into northern West Virginia's eroded, narrow valleys. Nothing was going to roll by, Wizard of Oz-style, but that didn't mean a tree wouldn't come down on the house.

I took Andy's hand and Shawn led us into the back basement.

"Okay, guys," he said. "Stay here." Then he turned and walked away as the wind outside gusted.

"Wait, where are you going?" I called. But I already knew the answer: he was securing his family in the safest spot in the house, tucking us into the stone foundation where nothing could suck us up or blow us out or fall and crush our skulls, and then he was going to stand in the yard and watch the tornado arrive. Because when potentially deadly weather arrives, Shawn wants to be front and center. He wants to see the sky turn green and the clouds rotate. You know those guys who stand on their decks and film the tornado as it goes by? And then, at some point in the video, a woman's voice shouts, "Get in here!" and the man reluctantly withdraws from his porch just as the twister tosses his lawn tractor in the pool? That's my husband.

"Come back!" I called. Andy tried to follow his dad. I grabbed his collar.

"But Daddy is out there," he whined.

"The sky is green!" Shawn shouted, the way you might shout, "I need two!" when you see the beer guy at a football game.

The man loves wind of any kind. We rode out the bands of Hurricane Rita one year on vacation. He spent that week on the porch, staring at the Gulf of Mexico and reporting hourly wind speeds. He loves blustery nights at home, too. The windows in our old house offer all the insulating protection of an aged swiss cheese. Outside, the wind roars through the trees, but within the home, we hear it scream around the corners in a high-pitched, banshee wail. Shawn shushes us when the shrieking gets especially loud so we can all hear it. He stays up late and listens to it howl while he plays a gory video game with a high startle factor. Every half hour, he ducks outside to see if anything noteworthy is flying by.

His joy is inversely proportional to my misery. I hate the wind. I'd sooner drive to Walmart at three o'clock in the morning and watch them restock the shelves than lie in bed and listen to it howl. I have a white noise machine to drown it out. And I sure as hell won't go outside on a windy night because I'm pretty sure something might get me. Wind stirs the imagination as much as the leaves.

In more rational moments, my hatred of wind extends beyond fear. It also irritates me, and I'm not alone in this. Apart from sailors and wind farmers, wind drives most of us berserk. In a 2019 *LitHub* piece titled "A Brief Eerie History of How the Wind Makes Us Crazy," Lyall Watson considers the differences in the ways men and women react to wind.

> Most women, very sensibly, seek shelter from the wind. But there is something about an approaching gale that makes men very restless. Almost as though the sight of swiftly-driven cloud or the sound of air rushing through the trees were stimuli that triggered some deep-seated response. . . . There is no doubt that days with a lot of wind were once dangerous ones, destroying

**The Value of Wind**

123

shelters, dispersing warning scents, and masking the sound of an approaching predator. And it may well be that, even in our modern microclimates, men in particular are still excited and disturbed by the old signals.

Studies indicate our behavior is indeed influenced by wind. Forty years ago, social psychologists Jonathan M. Charry and Frank B. Hawkinshire studied the effects of positive ions on human behavior. Blustery winds may strip electrons from otherwise neutrally charged elements in the air—oxygen, carbon dioxide, and nitrogen. An abundance of positive ions has been linked to tension, irritability, and slowed reaction times. Physical symptoms including nausea, migraine, and respiratory problems were noted, particularly in Israeli studies.

Many cultures have notorious winds. Chinooks plague the Pacific Northwest. The Andes Mountains in Argentina endure the zonda. Libyans suffer the ghibli; the Israelis, the sharav. The foehn torment Western Europe. And the despised Santa Ana winds bring nothing but misery for the residents of Southern California.

In her 1967 essay "The Santa Ana," Joan Didion wrote about the eponymous winds that haunt and torment the people of Southern California every year. The hot, dry gusts are known as "devil winds" for their tendency to exacerbate wildfires at speeds of forty miles per hour. They can trigger heavy fog and high surf in coastal areas, and, like many researchers and writers, Didion noted their unfavorable impact on those living in their path:

> There is something uneasy in the Los Angeles air this afternoon, some unnatural stillness, some tension. What it means is that tonight a Santa Ana will begin to blow, a hot wind from the northeast whining down through the Cajon and San Gorgonio Passes, blowing up sandstorms out along Route 66, drying the hills and the nerves to flash point. For a few days now we will see smoke back in the canyons, and hear sirens in the night. I have neither heard nor read that a Santa Ana is due, but I know it, and almost everyone I have seen today knows it too. We know it because we feel it.

There is indeed a correlation between the behavior of Southern Californians and the devil winds. *Los Angeles Magazine* noted a 30 percent increase in domestic abuse reports to the Santa Ana PD during a Santa Ana wind event. The purported reaction to ill winds may be tied to the brain itself. An Austrian study found low serotonin levels in subjects suffering from wind-related malaise. (Serotonin is a neurotransmitter that, in abundance, triggers good feelings.) In their 1981 study, Charry and Hawkinshire wrote, "Epidemiological data indicate that increased small positive air ionization due to changing weather conditions is associated with increases in industrial and automobile accidents, suicide, and crime as well as depression, irritability, and interference with central nervous system (CNS) function." Many of the reported symptoms occurred in subjects who were described as having a less resilient autonomic nervous system.

If we follow this thread, we'll discover a personality trait called "sensory processing sensitivity" (SPS), identified by psychologist Elaine N. Aron in the nineties. A person with high SPS is known as a Highly Sensitive Person (HSP), and somewhere around 20 percent of the population falls into this category. The HSP is a soul with an uphill battle in this world as they navigate around abrasive and overwhelming external stimuli. The difficulty stems from the very thing that makes them what they are—their sensitivity. The HSP is known for being sensitive to pain; easily overwhelmed by strong sensory input like bright lights, scratchy fabric, loud or harsh noises; needing to withdraw from time to time; easily startled; and negatively aroused by violence and chaos.

I am one of these Highly Sensitive Persons. (My husband would like to add that we also tend to get "hangry," a portmanteau of *hungry* and *angry* that transforms his affable partner into the human equivalent of a goat with its head stuck in a can.) I possess all the listed traits of an HSP, and I find nothing triggers my sensitivity more strongly than wind. While Shawn loves the constant stimulation of air-against-flesh, I find the wind physically unpleasant. An irritant. It feels like a cheese grater on my skin. The entire experience of a blustery day is overstimulating. My nerves fire in unison. Yet it goes beyond a physical sensation—the wind makes me angry. I look for a place to block the gusts—a rock or a building or even a tree trunk—anything to keep it off my skin. After half an hour exposed, I'm a rattlesnake, desperate to escape under a rock. Don't poke me unless you want your calf bitten.

**The Value of Wind**                                           **125**

I'm super cranky about indoor wind, too. Shawn loves fans, and I hate them. They make me nuts. It's like being smacked by a toddler repeatedly in the face, and the longer wind blows on me, the more I lose focus. I drift off in the middle of sentences and snap at my kids. The conflict follows us everywhere. He rolls the car windows down on the interstate and is perfectly content to ride along for hours with a cyclone of gas receipts and straw wrappers swirling around in the vehicle's cabin. He loves that heavy pressure on his cheeks. I couldn't hate the sensation more.

A driver cruising along with the windows open at fifty-five miles per hour is exposed to a continuous eighty-nine decibels of noise. That's enough to damage your hearing after eight hours; more than one hundred decibels—perhaps in a heavy traffic situation—can cause permanent damage in fifteen minutes. Not to mention the pollutants passengers inhale from vehicles around them. It's a price my husband is willing to pay. He loves wind that much.

So where does this leave a pair of souls like us? Partnership is about sharing a life, but it's equally about putting up with the fact that the other person isn't *you*. It's the most basic of concepts, because of course the other person isn't you, and that's a shame, because your life would be so much easier if the other person *was* you. You'd always know what you wanted for dinner. You'd never have to fiddle with the thermostat. And in my case, if I were married to me, I would never roll down the window on the interstate and invite insects into my mouth.

But when we share this life with another human—be they partner or sibling or child—we inevitably encounter these blustery points of contention, in which case someone has to give in and be somewhat uncomfortable. Who gets preference in the car window situation? The wind lover or the wind hater?

In such disputes, partners are supposed to use *I feel* statements for effective communication.

"*I* feel happy and comfortable when the wind from the interstate pounds my face."

"Well, *I* feel like there's a bug in my eye."

Ultimately, my husband always rolls up his window for my comfort. In turn, I don a jacket so he can crank the air conditioner until the moon roof freezes shut. It's a dance.

On a grander scale, my irritation pales in comparison to the potential for clean energy. The Allegheny Front, which runs down the eastern side of West Virginia, is one of the windiest places in the US and home to heavily logged forests of red spruce trees—the ones I tattooed on my hip. As global temperatures rise, the high-altitude, cold-loving species has no higher place to grow.

The red spruce in the highest of our high places stand as living proof of the ferocity of the Allegheny wind. You'll see them, branches flagged from the constant battery, on all the loftiest peaks. The wind is so strong and constant that the trees grow with it rather than against it (a metaphorical life lesson you and your cousin Ron should learn before Thanksgiving dinner erupts into another scalloped potato fight over COVID vaccines).

Thanks to the abundance of wind, there are currently 4 wind farms and 399 turbines turning in the blustery mountains of West Virginia. They're generating 2.7% of the in-state electricity and powering almost 160,000 homes. In 2019, wind power helped the state eliminate 2.4 million metric tons of $CO_2$ emissions, the equivalent of 520,000 cars. It also saved 1.5 billion gallons of water that would otherwise be used to generate electricity. A US Fish and Wildlife Service study determined that there was little danger to local bird populations from the turbines, though the technology is not without its detractors, who complain about everything from home values to the faint hum turbines produce.

People all over the world find reasons to hate wind turbines. Some claim the spinning blades trigger nausea. A recent executive-in-chief called them monsters. One fifty-five-year-old air traffic controller said he was getting headaches and insomnia whenever he was within a third of a mile of a turbine and the winds were blowing from the northwest. The apparent repercussions from this specific set of conditions? Two planes on his watch came within five hundred feet of a collision.

I don't admit this to everybody, but wind turbines hypnotize me. Of all the man-made things on earth I've been forced to look at, no others have brought me such childlike joy. I press my nose against the car window. I make squeaky noises. On our anniversary, we booked a rental on a lake in Maryland in the shadow of a wind farm. I didn't look at my phone once that weekend, nor did I pay much attention to my husband. As usual, when it comes to wind, we tolerate each other's fascinations.

Wind is tricky, but it does hold value. It offers part of the solution to our energy crisis. We can do something real and good with this freely available resource, but that doesn't mean it won't turn on us, twist itself into a black rage, and suck a llama right out of the barn. As usual, the human relationship with nature proves so multilayered that I get lost in its complexities. I can scream at the wind, and into it, but it's like being mad at fire even though it makes s'mores. And I must acknowledge, too, that nature's tools—fire, water, and wind—have shaped some of the places on earth I love the most, like the scoured face of West Virginia's Dolly Sods Wilderness and the ancient New River Gorge. These forces go where they will, with or without our consent, leaving us to rebuild from their devastation. Inventive creatures that we are, we've figured out how to hold back fire and water, to some extent. But we have no weapons against the wind, no tools for keeping it at bay. We can harness wind but never tame it. We can't put it out or dam it up. The wind can reach us in places where fire and water cannot. It blows through zippers and cracks, down chimneys and valleys, across river and rock. All we can do is hunker down against the mountain or beneath the earth, wait for it to pass, and hope it doesn't take us with it. Unless you're like Shawn, who's probably in the backyard right now, squinting at the sky, hoping to spot rotation.

# The Place We Belong, Described in Relatively Accurate Terms

On September 6, 1980, folk singer John Denver stood in the center of Mountaineer Field in Morgantown to mark the dedication of West Virginia University's new Milan Puskar Stadium. With his shaggy hair, round tinted glasses, and suede vest, he strummed his guitar and sang "Take Me Home, Country Roads" to a crowd of 50,000 people so spellbound they forgot their own names. The roaring mass of students and alumni stood, threw their arms around one another, and swayed back and forth like tent revivalists. Down on the field, the meanest-looking, bulldog linebackers melted into gelatinous blobs.

The song had done well when it was released nine years earlier, peaking at number two on the Billboard music charts and certifying gold the same year. You'll find covers of the song we call "Country Roads" by artists in Germany, France, Greece, India, Israel, Italy, Jamaica, Japan, Romania, Slovenia, Thailand . . . even Bangladesh. It showed up in *Fallout 76*, a post-apocalyptic video game set in West Virginia that my husband played obsessively. The song's appeal, of course, lies in the universal sense of place, whether that's a geographic location or a physical dwelling or a place of the heart and family. We all belong somewhere.

Artists who cover the song tinker with the lyrics to make it their own. Toots and the Maytals sing about West Jamaica in their cover, and Israel Kamakawiwo'ole pays homage to Hawaii's West Makaha in his. Ray Charles covered it. David Hasselhoff covered it. Sitcom characters Dwight Schrute and Andy Bernard sang it in an episode of NBC's *The Office*. WWE wrestler John Cena leads the crowd in song whenever he wrestles in the state. But even if no other artist ever breathed new life into "Country Roads," it would still be our most beloved paean.

Thanks to the song's incredible popularity, even those who have never visited our Mountain State know the lyrics that beg West Virginia's winding highways to lead the wandering singer home. When I discovered the karaoke bar on a Carnival cruise in college, the other West

Virginian in my class and I led the crowd in a rowdy chorus of discordant nostalgia for a place most of them had probably never been. And it didn't matter, because they all had a place they belonged, and as we bobbed about on the Caribbean Sea, those places felt so very far away, and we were all homesick together for a few moments.

To West Virginians, though, "Country Roads" is more than a hit from the seventies. We adopted the phrase "Almost Heaven" as our slogan, and the song was named an official state anthem in 2014. West Virginians are hypnotized by it, and John Denver has been our pied piper since he strummed the first chord.

West Virginians follow one rule above all others: When the song plays, we sing along. In fact, we agree to do so at birth. You know the birth certificates with the baby footprints? Well, here in the Mountain State, the fine print reads, "Per the location of their birth and the code set forth in the great state of West Virginia, the bearer of this foot agrees hence forth to cease all activity when 'Take Me Home, Country Roads' plays and to belt out, however tunelessly, the lyrics in an unabashed display of state pride, until the time of their death."

We keep the promise, though most young people leave West Virginia as soon as they can. The population continues to drop; we recently lost one of our congressional representatives after the US census revealed we're still shrinking. Many expats look back on the state with both disdain and regret. *We had to leave, they say. The economy sucked, and there aren't any jobs.* But even from their new homes, that song remains an unbreakable link to their birthplace. No matter where in the world they travel, "Country Roads" stops them in their tracks.

When I met my husband, who was born on West Virginia soil but raised across the river in Ohio, he shocked me by claiming he didn't like the song at all. I ruminated hard about committing to a man who loathed "Country Roads." It's like marrying someone who kicks bunnies for fun. He called the song "hee-haw shit." Shawn grew up listening to heavy metal, and his tastes evolved from bands like Van Halen to the kinds of bands led by shirtless, hirsute men who scream until their vocal cords rupture. It's so bad that our kids make him turn off his music before they reach school in the morning so their friends don't hear it.

But there's no escaping "Country Roads" for Shawn, because he moved back across the Ohio River, changed his residency, and proposed to a woman who plays it, loudly, on repeat. In the kitchen. In the car. Definitely on trips down said country roads. And she became a mountain mama to his children, one of whom is so deeply enamored with the song that he, too, asks for it to be played on repeat. When it's just Ben and me, we crank the volume up and howl.

Over time, though, Shawn started to come around, and I suspect it began at his first Mountaineer football game, where the song plays in every pregame show and again after a win. Even the hardest of hard rockers cannot withstand the emotion of tens of thousands of people falling momentarily in love with each other as they croon Denver's lyrics like a stadium full of blue and gold Care Bears. Granted, when I turn on his car, the radio is always set to heavy metal, and sometimes to a subgenre called death metal or a sub-subgenre called Swedish death metal. But he no longer complains when Ben and I play "Country Roads." Sometimes, I think his lips move.

Everyone in West Virginia grows up with the song. It played in the background of my childhood, as the soundtrack to school programs and assemblies, car trips, and July rides to the ice cream store in my dad's red Mustang. And though it's not the only famous John Denver song, and his greatest loves were Colorado and the Rocky Mountains, we look the other way on that, here.

In fact, we turn a blind eye to more than just Denver's state loyalties, because there's an undercurrent of controversy surrounding his greatest hit. I hate to bring it up; it's against the code. But as the story goes, when Denver heard an early version of the song for the first time, sitting with songwriters Taffy Nivert and Bill Danoff in Washington, DC, he loved it so much that he wanted it on his next album, even though he'd never crossed our border. West Virginia didn't inspire the lyrics— it was a road in Maryland and the DC region of the east. Nivert and Danoff had been driving on back roads and were thinking about country travel. Danoff said in a 2020 interview that he'd been remembering his childhood in western New England and rural family drives. Denver helped them finish the song in one night, and they knew they had a hit. And while West Virginians are prouder than a puffed-up chicken about the whole thing, we do have to reckon with the fact that the landmarks mentioned in the song don't represent our state very well. The Blue Ridge Mountains touch only a sliver of the easternmost part of the state, near Harper's Ferry. And the Shenandoah River, with its mellifluous name, flows through West Virginia for a brief twenty miles in the same region. Danoff admitted that he chose the Blue Ridge Mountains and Shenandoah River because they were "songwriter words." Both are redolent of western Virginia.

We hate being reminded of that. How could Denver have nailed it so perfectly without the song being about us? It's kind of like knowing your dog had a loving home before she was yours. You love your dog more than anything. She's *your* dog. She's part of your family. Your name is on her tag. When the vet scans her microchip, your name pops up as her owner. But there will always be a part of you that wonders if she would wag her tail if her former master came calling. And she would, of course, because she's a dog and she'd wag her tail at Hannibal Lecter if he stopped by for a snack.

Dogs love everybody, though, so you can live with that, and in some sort of situation where your dog was forced to choose, a little meat rubbed on your jawline would help her remember her loyalties. Sadly, we can't smear hamburger on our faces and lure in John Denver. So, we have to accept the fact that he and the songwriters didn't truly know us when they wrote about us, and that the final choice reportedly came down to two four-syllable states; the other was Massachusetts. Danoff said West Virginia sounded exotic and figured it probably had windy roads, so he picked us.

Geographically speaking, the Allegheny Mountains and the Greenbrier, Gauley, New, or Cheat Rivers would have been more appropriate references. He might even have chosen the North Fork of the South Branch of the Potomac River. But it's hard to imagine inebriated fans hollering those lyrics at a game. Then again, WVU students are known for setting their own couches on fire in the streets after a big win, so maybe I'm splitting hairs, here.

Regardless, there are always people who love to point out the song's geographical inaccuracies. We're irked when anyone mentions the fact that Denver, our musical champion, the man who tattooed West

Virginia onto international hearts and painted a golden picture of this place full of beauty and nostalgia, kind of got it wrong. We're the slightly uglier sister sent in place of the good-looking one who couldn't make it to the dance.

"We're so sorry, son. Melanie couldn't make it tonight. Would you mind if Myrtle went with you instead? Mind her psoriasis. It's finally starting to scab over."

But we love our anthem so much that we push these details away, and they only crop up when some non-West Virginian writes an article for *Southern Living* or the *Baltimore Sun*. And then we ask, why? Why point out the fly in our ointment? You know we need that ointment because we're usually wounded by some sort of black eye here, whether it's poverty, addiction, or flaky patches of peeling skin.

So, look, America, we *are* Myrtle. But if you'll just take us to the dance, you'll find out that we're fun and quirky and really good at catching trout and yes, setting couches on fire.

# The Pursuit of Everything

My family doesn't like traveling with me. They say I'm complicated. Controlling. Even exuberant bordering on manic. Because I want to see everything before I die.

Everything.

Each travel day is a puzzle. Every hour should fit perfectly, and any empty space can be packed with extras. Extra views, extra hikes, extra sunset photos. Have an unexpected twenty minutes? Run to the top of the hill and check out the scenery. The sun has set but the sky is still light? Grab a fly rod and head to the river. There's room for more. We can always do more.

While I see these calculating moves as an elegant pursuit of recreational efficiency, my family does not. They say I'm tense. Most people unwind and slow down on vacation, and my husband's family certainly did. Shawn's dad was a coal miner who died young—God knows he earned his time off. They worked hard all year and took a summer beach vacation during which they bobbed in the ocean, ate fried food, and dozed in beach chairs. It was the standard week of relaxation that most American families enjoy.

West Virginians often spend a week at Myrtle Beach, the Outer Banks, or Ocean City, as his family did. But in my family, we didn't take vacations. We took *trips*. I began to realize the distinction when I was nine years old, on a two-week visit to Yellowstone and the Tetons. My dad wanted us to see as much as possible. Six months before we left, he handed me guidebooks for the parks, told me to read them in their entirety and circle anything I wanted to do with a red pen. I circled everything.

On that trip, Dad woke us up at seven, and we piled into the car with the day's adventure not only plotted but booked in advance the previous fall. We had a specific route to drive each day, with no chance for a return to the hotel. We planned our movements down to the hour when a specific geyser might erupt—to maximize the number of eruptions we'd see—and squeeze in a few hours of fishing, a trail ride, and a picnic.

We covered a hundred miles and crawled into our beds exhausted, only to do it again the next day.

We saw everything we possibly could on these trips. And I never knew there were people out there who *didn't* yearn to see everything, who slept in and missed a sunrise gathering of elk in an alpine meadow or stayed up for a midnight Milky Way viewing in the desert. I never knew there was another way to experience the world, and it didn't matter because sitting in a lounge chair wasn't an experience anyway. It was a waste of time.

When I married Shawn, he wasn't prepared for the way his new wife would vacation. Like most honeymooners, he thought we'd sit by the pool, enjoy romantic dinners, and sip daiquiris together as the sun went down. But he was terribly wrong. I was not going to fly all the way to Hawaii just to sit on my wedded ass in a chlorinated cocktail bar. I allotted us one half-day of poolside relaxation so our bodies could adjust to the time change. We had drinks and rode the waterslide, and then I told him to get dressed because we had things to see. For the next ten days, we bodysurfed with turtles, swam with dolphins, hiked a volcano, snorkeled a reef, trekked through a canyon, sailed on a catamaran, kayaked up a river, climbed a waterfall, and ate a roasted pig. By the end, Shawn was in physical and mental shock.

Perhaps he thought I'd mellow over time, but I got worse over the decades. When we visited Yellowstone with our boys, we left West Virginia long before dawn. At 11 a.m. Mountain Time, we descended into Jackson Hole, toward the Tetons. I elbowed my husband awake so he wouldn't miss it.

"Wake up!" I said. "Look at those mountains!" He peered out through the slits in his eyelids, grunted in a *fuck-off* kind of way, and went back to sleep, content to miss an amazing view. I woke the children from their own comas to see their first glimpse of the Rocky Mountains, and I made them continue looking out their windows as we landed. *Made* them. As in, *You will look out that window at that mountain, young man, because this is a damned wonder of the natural world, and I don't care if you're tired and you have to pee. Unless you're bleeding out, you will stare at those Tetons. And work on your awe because I'm not buying it.*

I behaved similarly in a field in Townsend, Tennessee, later that summer as we stared up at the "Great American Eclipse" of 2017. I'd made plans for that trip a year in advance. Every move was plotted down to the minute, with backup plans in case clouds moved in. I was so wired I could barely sit in my skin. I had one chance to see the eclipse in Great Smoky Mountains National Park. *One chance.*

Everything fell into place on that bluebird day, and when totality came, we had a minute and a half to remove our protective glasses and stare up at it. After thirty-five seconds, seven-year-old Ben looked away to ask me a question, and I roared at him.

"Mom, could you—"

"*Look at the eclipse!*" I shouted. "*Just look at it!*"

Poor Ben. Will he remember the most remarkable cosmic event of his lifetime, or will he remember his wild-eyed mother barking at him during its apex? What if he'd been trying to tell me a snake had latched onto his foot? *Hey Mom, could you get this mamba off my toe and . . . oh, sorry. I'll just keep looking up.*

I really just want us to see everything.

Sometimes, my life feels like an episode of the *Twilight Zone* where the whole world has changed, but I'm the only one who realizes it, and I wonder if I'm out of tune or if it's the rest of you. I look at your vacation photos on the beach, and I want to smack you all. Why are you just bobbing around in the pool with beers in your hands? Surely there's an experience you could be having beyond a lounge chair. My God, get up!

When I meet roadblocks, I get anxious. I feel bees swarming in my chest when my family sleeps in or doesn't want to take an extra two hours to drive to the top of a mountain and watch the sunset, because who wouldn't want to drive to the top of a mountain and watch the sunset? Each morning, I imagine hundreds of people already out on the road, ahead of me, seeing things I'm meant to see that day, as if such wonders might tarnish under the gaze of too many eyes. I never ask myself what will happen if I don't see those things, or what it would mean if I weren't the first person to jump off the dive boat or reach the Clingmans Dome overlook. I only know that missing something would be unforgivable.

A few summers ago, we went to the Allegheny Mountains on a ziplining and rock-climbing trip. But it didn't feel like enough—I also wanted to kayak and fish and go tubing. I wanted to ride a train up a mountain and hike back down. I wanted to walk through a bog and see West Virginia's last old-growth hemlocks.

"They're going to succumb to the invasive woolly adelgid," I told Shawn that first morning as I packed food for the day. "We *have* to see them."

"Why do you do that," he asked me. "Why do you have to see all the things?"

"YOLO, man," I said, citing the no-longer-cool acronym meaning *you only live once.*

But he said it wasn't YOLO at all—it was FOMO. FOMO stands for *fear of missing out*, and there's a big difference between the two. YOLO arises from the spirit of adventure, a desire to get out there and leap, trusting that the net will appear, as the naturalist John Burroughs promised it would. FOMO, however, is motivated by anxiety and fear, powerful tools for getting things done, perhaps stronger than the thrill of adrenaline. YOLO, Shawn said, would explain a desire to BASE jump off the New River Gorge Bridge, if I had one; it wouldn't explain my itch to start packing the car at six o'clock in the morning.

"You've got terrible FOMO," Shawn told me.

"I do *not* have terrible FOMO," I said, indignant. He made it sound like a nasty case of armpit fleas.

"You do," he said. "And you're out of control sometimes. Look at the boys. They're exhausted and it's the second day of our trip."

A Harvard Business School magazine article coined the term FOMO in 2004; the *Oxford English Dictionary* added it in 2013. The notion is heavily entwined with social media use. Whether it's an enviable vacation or the purchase of a new house, it's easy to feel jealous of others' experiences and inadequate by comparison. One study in *Psychiatry Research* reported a connection between social media use and smartphones, the results of which included anxiety and depression. FOMO's also been associated with boredom and loneliness.

But I had FOMO long before social media was born, so I'm not sure I can blame Facebook. My fear of missing out is rooted in a place far deeper than the digital world. I don't have to post about things—I have to *see* things. Wild things. Unspoiled things. Mountains and deserts and

Deep & Wild

brain coral. And I've always dragged my family along with me, whether they liked it or not.

"I know why you're like this," my husband said, a few weeks later. "It's because you're afraid of dying."

"Get the hell out of here," I said. But I thought about it for a few months, and I think he's right. I *am* afraid of dying. Everybody is, of course, but if I'm dead, I don't get to go back and see Hetch Hetchy, the lake that we missed in Yosemite because I miscalculated the amount of time we had to see it. Shawn said we'd catch it on the next trip; I worried there wouldn't be a next trip. The planet is deteriorating, and I haven't seen wild kiwis yet. I haven't dived in Palau or hiked to Mount Everest base camp.

I suppose it's all rather silly, because when I'm dead, I'll be able to visit these places in spirit form, which is not only far cheaper but also eliminates earthly discomforts like traveler's diarrhea and those pesky pickpockets. Conversely, if it turns out there's nothing after death, I won't give a hoot that I missed the tree-kangaroos of Papua New Guinea anyway. But while I'm alive, I still want to see everything, even if it means gastrointestinal paroxysms in the Khumbu Valley.

So maybe it's Fear of Death. I've got FOD, which is its own kind of FOMO. Fear of missing out on life. On being alive. And I wonder if this condition is a demon to exorcise or an encouraging spirit. Is it hurting me or leading me onward?

Perhaps both.

The first summer of the pandemic, we took a West Virginia vacation, staying local to avoid the dangers of travel. It wasn't an extravagant or long trip, just a week in the mountains that culminated beside the Greenbrier River. The puzzle pieces were harder than usual to fit into place under the very real threat of COVID-19. We needed isolated rentals. We needed to avoid restaurants and grocery stores. I accepted the challenge and put that trip together like a handcrafted jigsaw masterpiece. I printed the final itinerary in bold ink (I stopped short of laminating it, because I'm not a nut, and because I didn't have a laminating machine) and stored it with the maps in the car.

Per the itinerary, we'd arrive at the Greenbrier River rental cabin on Sunday at 6 p.m., and we did. We relaxed on Monday. Tuesday's intended activity was a trip to Sandstone Falls on the New River, a spot I'd always wanted to see, where the kids could swim. I was excited, but I knew everyone would first need those twenty-four hours of relaxation to unwind after several days of what had become known as "Mom's aggressive fun." We'd seen and done some neat stuff, like tubing in the South Branch of the Potomac and spotting a rare timber rattlesnake. But the kids were sick of the windy roads and Dramamine, and they were tired of getting in and out of the car. I'd anticipated this, hence the scheduled day off. It was going to be a great afternoon of lounging by the river. They would need to recharge if we were going to kick it back into high gear the following day for more adventuring.

Relaxation Day was glorious. We floated in the shallows of the Greenbrier in clear, warm water. The kids caught crawdads; Shawn caught smallmouth. We tubed. I brought my camp chair out into the current and sat with my feet suspended in the stream. The sun shone down on us, and nobody moved beyond the three hundred feet of river in front of the cabin. We agreed that it was one of the best days ever.

"What's going on tomorrow?" Andy asked at dinner that evening.

"Yeah, do we get to relax again tomorrow?" Ben asked. "Or are you making us get up and go somewhere again?" They looked cautious but hopeful.

"I was thinking we'd go see Sandstone Falls," I started. Their faces fell. "It's really cool, though, guys. It's the widest waterfall in West Virginia and you can swim and—"

"How far is it?" Andy asked.

"About an hour," I said.

He looked down at his food and sighed. Nobody said anything. A cloud of tension puffed back into the room. I assured my family that they could sleep in and promised we'd just *mosey* on down to Sandstone Falls when we got going in the morning. (I often use the word "mosey" when I really mean "haul ass.")

I woke up the next morning before the fog had lifted. As I drank my coffee by the river, the day ahead tugged at my attention. We had no cell service, so I couldn't review the latest forecast, check for possible detours, or time out the drive, though I'd already done so many times. I just had to sit there by the water, away from the house to keep my promise not to wake the guys. I knew they'd be up by 8:30, since the day before had been a lazy, restful one.

They were not. Eight-thirty came and went. Nine. By ten, I'd checked on them three times to see if anyone was stirring. Nobody was. The buzzing in my chest began. We were missing things.

Shawn appeared at the coffee pot at 10:17 a.m.

"Man, I got some good sleep," he said, yawning. "What time did you wake up?"

"About 5:45," I said. His face shifted into worry.

"Oh no. You must be going nuts." He took big sips of coffee and tried to shake himself awake. Experience had taught him that while his wife would appear to be methodically preparing for the day, each loud exhalation brought her head one step closer to physically separating from her body, rolling across the floor, and sinking its teeth into his ankle. Because she needed to see everything.

My husband had told me a dozen times that I couldn't see *all* the things before I died. But on some irrational level, I thought I could figure out a way. The alternative was too much to accept. *Me, dead.* Having never seen Sandstone Falls. Not one of the eight wonders of the world, but maybe one of the eight wonders of West Virginia. To be so close to the falls and not take advantage of the opportunity . . . it was torture. What was going to happen if I didn't get to see them?

For the first time, I asked the question of myself. What *would* happen?

The answer was that I'd miss out on something. I might die and leave it unseen, undone. It felt unbearable. And yet it felt inevitable.

"Okay," Shawn said, glugging his coffee to ingest as much caffeine as he could and wincing as it scalded its way down his esophagus. "What's the plan?" From his bed, Ben shouted at his video game, while Andy slept in deep silence. My husband offered me a tentative smile, attempting to gauge my mood, which would in turn dictate how fast he forced himself and our kids into motion.

The day before had been so mellow. Nobody fought with anybody. Nobody had uttered a word of complaint. My kids had seen nothing beyond the view from the riverbank, and they told me it was one of the best days of their lives. When I asked them what they liked about it, Ben had said, "I liked catching crawdads with you, Mom. You were so funny." It was such an ordinary activity, one we could have done in the creek at home.

Shawn poured another cup of coffee. "I can get the kids up," he said. "I know you want to see Sandstone Falls. It's fine by us."

That was a lie, but it meant that my husband and kids loved me enough to drag their tired bodies and soggy brains out onto the winding West Virginia roads so I could see more things.

In that moment, I saw myself for what I was: scared of something intangible, something I had no control over. I was the problem, holding on so tightly that the joy—mine and theirs—was oozing out between my fingers and slipping away. I hated the thought, and as I weighed it against the FOMO bubbling up in my gut, the scales tipped. A little.

"I think we should just stay here today," I said, though it pained me to do so. "Yesterday was perfect, so let's do it again."

"Are you sure?" he asked.

I took another minute to consider what I might do if I had one day to live. Would I want to be in the car with my exhausted family, racing to see a few more sights, none of which would ever be enough to satisfy my FOMO? Or would I want to watch the morning fog lift beside a West Virginia trout stream and play in its warmth with the three people I loved most?

"Let's skip it," I said. "Sandstone Falls isn't going anywhere." As I said it, I realized I actually believed it. The boys were overjoyed by another lazy day, and we'd look back on those forty-eight hours on the Greenbrier River as the most memorable of the three-year pandemic.

I finally saw Sandstone Falls, almost four years later, with a friend. The placid New River, fifteen hundred feet wide where it tumbled over crumbling ledges of soft rock, marked the southern gateway to the newly designated New River Gorge National Park and Preserve and the beginning of its transformation into West Virginia's iconic mountain whitewater. A unique riverside flat rock plant community, found in only a few places in the state, grew along the shoreline. I spent a contented hour watching the water, smelling the moss, and crawling along the boulders.

My family stayed home, and not only did they lose no sleep over the missed opportunity, but they reported a solid night of rest and fantastical dreams about winning lottery tickets, baskets of kittens, and the world's largest Marshmallow Peep.

I'd completed the journey, for myself. And yet, I've not fully figured out how to let go of my FOMO. This isn't a Hallmark movie that ends when the protagonist sees the light and turns her life around. I might have had a come-to-Jesus moment, but it wasn't an exorcism. I'm still me, I still want to cheat death, and I still want to see everything. I know I won't, and it sucks. But I force myself to take a breath and remember that everything will be there tomorrow, waiting for me.

And if it isn't, today will have to do.

# It Never Snowed

Northern Appalachian winters suck. The sun hides behind what a friend calls "the monocloud"—the low layer of steel stratus clouds packed so tightly that you can't tell where one ends and another begins. They're a shitty swath of gray frosting atop a soggy, brown cake, because West Virginia's verdant green cover dies months prior. Sometimes winter bathes us in a dreary, forty-degree rain; other times it chews our faces with subzero teeth, the kind of nips that turn a nose tip black and burst a pipe at two o'clock in the morning, when I seek insulation levels somewhere between summit day on Mount Everest and the Stay-Puft Marshmallow Man.

Winter's blessing is snow, and a little bit of white fluff dresses up the dark, gray landscape. But now, fewer and fewer snowstorms drop their frozen manna. The past seven years have been the warmest in recorded history, and the winter of 2022-2023 fell in step. Only one snowfall lit up the long stretch of our dark days.

We measure snow on the highest West Virginia ridges in feet, but the northern panhandle gets very little accumulation, and storms rarely produce impressive results. And yet, every year, some sensational system comes along, looking for all the world like it's going to dump on us. A few days out, weather people start predicting snow totals of five to ten inches. *Hell yes*, we shout. As the storm takes shape, totals increase. Hold onto your frozen hams, the weather people say, because it's looking more like eight to twelve and this beast is going to wallop us! The kids toss their homework out the window, and the adults scurry off to Lowe's to buy shovels, which they use to bludgeon other shoppers so they can get to the last few bags of rock salt. My husband wheels out the snow blower. He pokes valves and revs the engine in a roaring test run, announcing every few minutes that he's "got 'er ready to go." And the National Weather Service flashes accumulation maps on every screen—six to twelve, starting at 4 p.m., so leave work early because it's gonna be a roaring shit show, people. Snow's coming and hell's coming with it.

In the final hours, though, the storm starts to wobble, and the weather forecasters do, too. Welp, they say, this thing is shifting a little, and it looks like the northern panhandle of West Virginia is now back in the four- to six-inch range. Okay, probably three to five. But we *could* get up to a foot or more of snow. So make with the bread and milk, folks. Get to the store and start throwing elbows.

Inevitably, at T-minus two hours, a sudden swath of warm air materializes. Nobody knows where it came from—weather forecasting is complicated, people. We're doing our best, go spread your rock salt and let us do our jobs. And by the way, there's the *slightest* chance that the warm air aloft will cause a *little bit* of mixing, just a *brief period* of freezing rain, and then we *swear* it's going to switch over to snow and you're still going to die, we promise. And the adults get even more verklempt because freezing rain means a layer of ice on tree branches and power lines, which means the potential for power outages, which, yes, does mean we might freeze to death, but more importantly, the god damned internet will go down and the kids will turn on us like circus tigers. We open a dusty cabinet and root around to see if there are any board games in there, find only Yahtzee and an unopened Big Boggle, and look at each other in horror. This discovery leads us to a second cabinet—the liquor cabinet—which has been stocked for weeks. Out of an abundance of caution, of course.

At T-minus one hour, the weather people do an about-face and announce that accumulation will reach ten to fourteen inches! The radar map is a swath of blue. The first few tentative flakes begin to fall, so fine they look like tree pollen. And we shout, "Kids! It's happening!" And the kids scream, and we stand on the porch and wait for the big, honking snow blobs to start smacking us in the face.

And that's when we hear *plink. Plink plink. Splat.* The snow is making noise when it lands, which is impossible because snow is fluffy and quiet and what the hell is making that plinking sound and *oh my God it's not snow—it's sleet.*

Aside from that time God rained flaming hail down on Egypt, sleet is the worst kind of precipitation. It's cold and wet, and it bombs the ground with *plinks* and *plops*. It forms a white layer across the grass like a soggy spiderweb, and it ruins the chance for any subsequent snow accumulation. Sleet is a snow killer.

The radar shows solid blue over the whole Ohio Valley, except for West Virginia's northern panhandle, which is Pepto Bismol pink, an island of sleet amidst a cascade of snow. As the hours pass, the pink blob changes shape over us and rearranges itself but refuses to move on. It's parked over us, National Weather Service says, and it looks like the panhandle is going to have "significantly lowered totals of snow," maybe one to two inches at the most.

All that preparation, all the excitement and anticipation—the effort it took to whack that old man with an ergonomic shovel—was for nothing. The news shows nearby Pittsburghers buried up to their thighs and kids romping around in the streets. Powder is dumping down on the ski resorts. And in our yard? Sad slush puddles. In the morning, we load our kids into the car and drive them to school. They slam the doors and stomp off to their classrooms as sleet squirts out from beneath their boots.

This happens so often that we know better than to get excited, but it doesn't stop the kids from digging out their sleds, *just in case*. And when they do, I have a moment of dread. Memories of those let's-play-in-the-snow years trigger a piercing angst, because dressing small children for winter play is a freak show. It starts with the layering of shirts. When you put the second one on, the sleeves of the first shirt get shoved up to the kid's armpits. So you reach up under the second sleeve to pull the first one down. But his sleeves are so tiny that your hand doesn't fit up there, so you need his help.

"When I put this sweatshirt on, I want you to hold your sleeves with your fingers," you say. Not that it matters, because he won't. Still, this pales in comparison to the donning of snow pants, which itself is a million times easier than wedging tiny feet into boots.

"Point your foot. No, *point* it, Ben. Like *this*. See what I'm doing with my foot? No, *point* it! Is your foot in there? Can you feel the end of the boot with your toe? What's wrong with your sock? Is it wrinkled? Hang on, let me take the boot off. Just lean on me. No, lean on my shoulder. Don't bite me. No, I said we're taking the boot *off*, now. Yes, you still get to go outside. No, not in your socks. *Please* just work with me."

The misery of the boots is, in turn, a romp in the park compared to the stuffing of small hands into mittens or gloves, which, on the horror scale, lands somewhere between root canal and being eaten alive by ants.

"Oh my God—I keep telling you, hold your hand out! Like *this*! Well, now you've got two fingers in one hole. Pull it out. *Fuck*, now the lining is inside out! Yes, I know I said fuck. Don't say fuck, Ben. That's not a nice word. We don't say fuck. No, I don't think your friends at preschool know that word."

Logic *should* play a part in this ritual. In a tired parent's mind, the effort expended to dress the child needs to be proportional to the amount of snow on the ground. That, in turn, should be related to the amount of fun the child will have. To our grown-up way of thinking, more snow equals more fun equals justifiable parental effort. It takes a damn fine snowfall to make it worth the time and energy we'll spend on dressing the child. But a mere dusting excites the kid. Even wretched sleet sends him into a frenzy of begging. *Pleeeeaze? Puh-leeeeeeze, Mommy? Please can I go play?* And of course you acquiesce, because he's your child and it's snow and you have such fond memories of your own snow days. So you take a deep breath, grit your teeth, and stuff him into his gear until you're sweating like a sow and kicking yourself for not taking that job in Florida when you had the chance.

And you're exhausted. You spent twenty-five minutes getting him dressed, twelve more getting him undressed when he realized he had to pee, and then nineteen more getting him re-dressed. But like childbirth or remodeling a kitchen, you forget the agony of it all the minute you see his face as he stares up at the snow-laden spruce and tumbles down the sliding board into a fluffy snow pile. His joy melts your frustration and, for the seven minutes you're outside before he loses his glove and starts whining for hot chocolate, you're in love—with your child, with his wonder, with winter and its beautiful gift.

Then his exposed hand goes numb, and the dog knocks him down, and the whole thing ends with his wet clothing strewn about and his tongue burned because he insisted on drinking his hot chocolate before it was cool, even though you said, "This is hot. It will burn your tongue." You warned the little snow potato, but now he's crying on the floor for several reasons: he's soggy, his mouth hurts, and elephants don't fit in locomotives.

**Deep & Wild**

Those tiresome years have passed in my house, and now the boys only come out if there's sled-worthy snow, which happens less and less. They do, however, appreciate ice hikes, and we know where to find ice. My family bought a little cabin on a lake in the seventies. It's a summer place, but the lake freezes each January during a predictable cold snap. Most years, there's at least a few days when we can walk on it, and my dad and I look forward to the annual tradition.

According to the DNR of Minnesota—who probably knows better than anyone—ice four inches thick will support the weight of an average person. Eight inches will hold a snowmobile. Thirteen to fifteen inches will support a medium-sized truck.

Dad's formula for safe ice-walking is a bit cruder, but it's based on over fifty years of observation. According to his Generally Nonspecific Rules of Ice That You Should by No Means Take as Gospel (nor am I responsible if you do something stupid), three or four days of subfreezing temps will freeze the entire lake and you can walk on the ice if you stay near the shore. After several weeks of below-freezing temperatures, the lake is safe to cross—go where you will. At a month or so, ice fishing huts will appear. And after two or three months of temps in the teens, you'll start to see tire tracks on the lake. Go ahead and set up camp. Bring a chair, crack a beer, and make friends with Big Curtis in the saugeye shack next door because that ice is going to stick around for a very long time.

That's not a bad thing, because frozen lakes appeal to kids, in particular. If you can get them to put down their devices, they'll realize there's nothing cooler than stomping around, sliding along, and chucking rocks. My kids are first-rate chuckers. In fact, if there's one thing you can count on most any human being to do, it's hurl a rock onto the ice. We may say we do it to test the thickness, but I think some primal urge compels us. It's common in adolescent males, who will spend a whole afternoon throwing rocks. My boys spent sixty minutes on the task one afternoon, and when they launched their first stones, a high-pitched pinging split the frozen air. It was the same soprano song those plastic bird water whistles from the 1980s made (toys eBay describes as *vintage* just to hurt my feelings, I think). My sons had discovered Ralph Waldo Emerson's "ice-harp," which he described in his journal on December 10, 1836.

It Never Snowed

A thin coat of ice covered a part of the pond, but melted around the edge of the shore. I threw a stone upon the ice which rebounded with a shrill sound, and falling again and again, repeated the note with pleasing modulation. I thought at first it was the "peep, peep" of a bird I had scared. I was so taken with the music that I threw down my stick and spent twenty minutes in throwing stones single or in handfuls on this crystal drum.

Emerson was a chucker, too.

This is acoustic dispersion, i.e., the ice-harp. As sound waves move through the ice, the high frequency wavelengths travel faster than the low frequency ones. This accounts for the chirping sound. In my unprofessional experience, that sound means the ice is untrustworthy. I don't walk on ice that *pings*. (The dogs do, but that's why I take at least two. I've got my ice-testing dog and my spare dog. They're like birth control—it never hurts to double up because nobody wants an unexpected swimmer.)

During the brutal winter of 2015, temperatures in the Ohio Valley plunged to record lows. It was the first time most of us had ever heard the term "polar vortex." Cold air came down from the Arctic in January and covered the eastern half of the country. The jet stream locked the pattern into place well into March and produced extreme freezing temperatures, even in the South. It was so frigid in January that two baby African penguins at Pittsburgh's National Aviary had to go inside. The trend continued in February with life-threatening cold. Over 600 records were set for low temps in the eastern half of the country. Lake Erie was 94% iced over that winter; Lake Superior was 80% covered. The ice on our lake lasted from January until April. It was almost three feet thick and could have supported a fleet of Hummers.

The next year, spring came early to kick off one of the hottest years on record. The lake freezes less and less as climate change softens our once-white winters into earth tones. We still get one good ice walk per year, but the shift is noticeable. March no longer feels like winter. The earth smells wet and heavy as the earliest signs of spring peek out: daffodil leaves and forsythia buds, both of which have been arriving weeks earlier than they used to. February isn't their time, but there they are, just as we shouldn't be hiking in January without hats and gloves. But there we are. It feels disjointed and wrong, and yet it's hard to wish away warmth and light and life.

Until recently, it was easy to miss those encroaching signs of climate change as they crept across West Virginia. These new summer weather events can easily be dismissed as just another dry season, or an especially rainy one. Patterns of precipitation in June, July, and August don't necessarily strike us as warning signs because we remember the great drought of '88 (which continued into '89 and ranked as the worst since the Dust Bowl), and the five hundred-year flood of 2004 when Hurricane Ivan stalled over the upper Ohio Valley and caused catastrophic flooding we hadn't seen in our lifetimes. Most of us can't even describe the specific effects of El Niño or La Niña on our area (does it get wetter and cooler or hotter and drier?), though we've had many such seasons. We aren't good at recognizing long-term trends on their own, and summer is too busy a time to look for them. Mild winters, however, defy our childhood recollections. We remember frequent snowfalls, hours outside with frozen glove tips and red rashes on our faces from the stabbing wind on the sledding hill. Gen Xers recall "big dumps" like the Blizzard of 1993, but I don't think my kids—Gen Z—have ever seen a big dump. This past year, I didn't bother to buy Ben new boots.

These warm winters wave their arms like six-year-olds trying to get our attention. *Hey! Mom! Look what I'm doing! Do you see me? Mom? Are you watching? Maaaaahm! Watch me!* And when we do, we see our skis stowed in the garage, sleds stacked and dusty. We see day lilies and robins and daffodils when we should be cursing the groundhog as he dives back into his burrow for six more weeks. And we think back to the white winters we knew and try to grasp the enormity of the swing, even as we shed layers and comment on what fantastic weather we're having.

It's happening fast, and it's happening weird. After the balmy March of 2022, a snowstorm blew in on April 19. The hummingbirds had just arrived, and the deck furniture was out. Our magnolia blossoms froze to death because they thought it was safe to flower. Three days later, the mercury climbed to seventy-five. A year later, the winter of 2023 was one of the three warmest on record.

And it never snowed.

Nature can't keep up with the changes we've wrought. Our kids will face an extreme world of climate catastrophes, and our grandkids may face dystopian hardship and hunger we invent in young adult novels. It triggers an overwhelming existential dread. It also triggers sorrowful nostalgia in the non-panicked moments. They'll never know frozen winters. They'll never know three feet of snow. They'll never drag their children in a faded orange sled across the middle of the lake, step by aching step, exhausted and sweaty from the fight to stuff said progeny into puffy down suits. They'll never watch the TV in anxious prayer for school cancellation and scream out holy hallelujahs when the word goes out. They'll never perform the rites, the snow rituals their parents have carried out a hundred times, predictably, when days get short. And we'll wonder how any child can call their life full if they haven't clomped through a hushed, sparkling forest in ill-fitting moon boots with a ratty hand-knit scarf trailing on the ground.

Of course, it won't matter to them. They can't feel the loss of something they've never had. Those memories will never form, never exist in their hearts or photo albums. They won't know what they're missing.

And we will.

# The Flat Earth

I t's taken me forty years, but I've finally realized something: I don't like flat things.

Okay, that's not entirely true. I don't dislike *all* flat things. I'm fine with flat-assed people because I'm one of them and couldn't grow a rounded apple booty if I did a thousand squats a day. I also think a kitchen floor should be nice and flat (as opposed to mine, which lists to the north, something you become keenly aware of when you upend a glass of orange juice and it makes a sloppy, sideways dash for the refrigerator's undercarriage). And I think a dock should be flat, because the lake is cold in March, and it's a lot easier to appreciate that fact when you're not in it.

But when it comes to land, flat throws me off, and a lot of West Virginians feel this way. If there's one thing we have in common, it's a complete absence of flat land beneath our feet. We know nothing but inclines, declines, cliffs, and edges, and that topography comforts us. We don't know what to make of flat because we have no flat. In fact, for many of us—including me—flat is unsettling. It feels like a blank stare. Unreadable. I need some contrast to help categorize the world around me.

Even a rolling landscape isn't enough to bring me any peace. I drove through northern Illinois once, where the countryside wanders up and down at a gentle grade. I could see the horizon off in the distance, and I felt weird—was this some kind of prairie-hill hybrid? Likewise, my mom grew up in the pastoral suburbs of Philadelphia. She loved the rolling countryside, but when we visited, the area confused me. What's with the lumps in the ground, I wanted to ask. They were like mountains that couldn't get up enough steam and just gave up on themselves. I wanted to waggle my finger at the undulations and tell them if they'd tried a little harder, they'd at least be hills.

I understand that our country consists of a wide variety of terrains, and this is what makes it so diverse and visually appealing. Ocean lovers find their place, as do desert people and great northern woods people. And there are the flat landers, too. But I'm not the only one weirded-out by a lack of relief. A 2016 article in the *New Yorker* by Larissa MacFarquhar examined voters in our state. The focus was on how West Virginia moved from blue to red in the last two decades, but it also addressed the unique love West Virginians have for the land beneath our feet, not in defiance of its extremes but because of them.

She wrote, "Many people talk about a connection to the ground itself. West Virginia doesn't look quite like any other place—hardly any flat land, because the densely wooded hills are crushed so close together there's barely room for a road between them—and its confining closeness forms a kind of physical bond between people who find it familiar."

She went on to quote a West Virginia newspaper publisher named Ed Martin, who said, "When I'm in California, I feel like something bad's going to happen, because there's so much empty space. Here it's cozy. If you believe the mountains are yours, like most West Virginians do, when you get back to these mountains you feel comfortable again. You feel at ease."

I've driven through neighboring Ohio and felt the same way Mr. Martin does in California. As you cross the Ohio River and leave West Virginia, our tight, eroded hollows give way to wider hills and valleys, which in turn give way to fields. Corn pops up in every direction. The earth stretches on and on until it meets a perfectly level western horizon line.

And I don't like it. To echo Mr. Martin, I don't trust flat. Anything that seems simple and easy probably has something to hide. You have no idea what's out there. A tornado, a serial killer, some sort of Japanese kaiju monster . . . there's nowhere to hide if one should appear. Anything with laser-beam eyes will see you immediately, and what are you going to do—hide behind that Mail Pouch Tobacco barn? King Ghidorah has *three* heads. At least one of them is going to spot you.

But in West Virginia, we've got giant walls of rock between us and the things that might get us. And yeah, in some places they're so close together we only see the sun between 11:50 a.m. and 12:15 p.m., but it's okay because skin cancer is on the rise and shade is a small price to pay for refuge from Godzilla's wrath. And I realize I'm probably being

Deep & Wild

ridiculous and more than a little petulant (I'm sorry, Ohio—it's not you, it's your topography), but I don't think I'm alone on this flat thing.

What can I say? I'm a mountain girl, and geology fascinates me. On road trips, I bring a geology guide to West Virginia so I can torment the kids by pulling over every seven miles to point at a cliff or anticline or rock formation and thumb through the pages to explain what they're seeing. Not that they're looking, because after the first eleven stops, they beg for the sedating relief of Dramamine and slip into a backseat coma, safe from their mother's rock hounding.

There are plenty of great books on the subject. George Constantz is a naturalist, environmental educator, and the author of *Hollows, Peepers & Highlanders: An Appalachian Mountain Ecology* in which he explains, for the layperson, the region's geologic history.

The Appalachian Mountains began to rise about 600 million years ago and reached their maximum height about 300 million years ago. Our mountains have been steadily eroding since Triassic time. Altogether, the Appalachian Mountains have been uplifted out of the ocean for more than 500 million years, making Appalachia one of the oldest terrestrial environments on earth. By comparison, today's great mountain ranges—the Andes, Himalayas, and Alps—are infants, merely 50 million years old.

Most of West Virginia lies on the Appalachian Plateau. This area was lifted uniformly in the Paleozoic Era and gradually recedes from 4,863 feet at Spruce Knob to less than 600 feet on the western edge of the state; on its eastern border, it peaks at the Allegheny Front and drops into the Ridge-and-Valley Province. This folded mountain belt runs the entire length of the Appalachians, varying in width from fourteen to eighty miles. The ridges run parallel to one another, as do the corresponding valleys. In some areas, they're squeezed tightly together, but the number of ridges doesn't change. Streams flow through each valley, coming together where breaks in the vertical earth allow. This is how we end up with named branches: the South Branch of the Potomac River runs through Pendleton County. One valley to the east flows the South Fork of the South Branch; one valley west is the North Fork of the South Branch. We've also got a North Branch of the Potomac and its tributaries.

While the eastern end of the Appalachian Plateau appears to be a ridge of high mountains, it's really the steep slope that creates this illusion. It's a big drop and, despite my adoration for and comfort in this landscape, one I've thought often about. A few years ago, we bought our first camper. It was a pop-up—very un-fancy, lightweight, and easy to tow behind my SUV. Neither my husband nor I had ever driven a trailer, so we had to learn. We drove it to a parking lot and took turns backing it up. Shawn managed to get the hang of it pretty quickly. I, on the other hand, did not. I tried all the methods. The most often suggested one was to put my hands at the bottom of the wheel and move them the way I wanted the trailer to go.

I jackknifed the camper. So, I tried another way—ooching along very slowly, turning the wheel one micro-degree at a time. I jackknifed the camper. Some people on my West Virginia Campers Facebook group suggested looking into the side mirrors as I backed up and shouting "GO AWAY!" when I saw the trailer's reflection appear.

I jackknifed the camper. And by the ninth attempt, rather than admonishing the pop-up with a measured yet assertive, "GO AWAY," I spat out a searing "FUCK THIS SHIT!", jumped out of the car, and kicked a crumpled can of Iron City across the parking lot, which happened to belong to the local Catholic diocese. ("Thou shalt not mangle thy trailer." For those who need a refresher, that's from the book of Jayco, 3:19. King James version.)

I did eventually learn, sort of, to back up the camper. But I don't park it at campgrounds. Shawn does that, and he does it well, so I stand off to the side and shout constructively critical yet helpful things like "A little to the left!" and "Dammit, I said LEFT!" and "Sorry, sorry, my bad, I meant RIGHT, I'll go get a stick to scrape that squirrel off the tires." However, if we're ever in a pinch and need someone to throw a temper tantrum on Palm Sunday or back the pop-up into the Black Fork of the Cheat River, I'm ready to step in.

On one of our first trips with the pop-up, I booked a site at Seneca Shadows Campground in Pendleton County, at the foot of Seneca Rocks, one of West Virginia's most famous landmarks. The crag is a razorback ridge of exposed Tuscarora Quartzite that rises nine hundred feet above the valley floor. It's a popular spot for hikers and rock climbers. The campground sits across the valley and offers an impressive view of the rocks. I was ridiculously excited. And while the preparations for a four-hour drive and four days of camping with two kids and a dog sucked up a lot of mental energy, only one true obstacle stood out in my mind.

Allegheny Mountain.

The Allegheny Front is imposing as hell, and because it runs along the entirety of West Virginia's eastern mountains, there's no way to access Pendleton County, the eastern panhandle, or Virginia from the west without descending it. You've got nowhere to go but down, and Allegheny Mountain is the gatekeeper, the final boss that stands between travelers and Seneca Rocks, Spruce Knob, Cass Railroad, Green Bank National Radio Astronomy Observatory . . . all the West Virginia must-sees that grace postcards and T-shirts and bumper stickers.

And it's a monster.

US Route 33 crosses the Eastern Continental Divide at the Randolph/Pendleton County line and descends the Allegheny Front over the eponymous mountain. The road, which has been the sight of many accidents, winds around three sharp curves at a 10 percent grade. It's been called the most dangerous stretch of road in West Virginia. More than twenty serious wrecks have happened in the last fifteen years, and several people have died, including the driver of a runaway tractor trailer and the uphill traveler whose car the out-of-control rig sliced in half. According to newspapers, trucks have gone "into the ravine" at all three curves—Dead Woman's Curve, Horseshoe Curve, and a third, unnamed curve—but anyone who has descended Allegheny Mountain will tell you it's not a ravine at all.

It's a cliff.

Over the years, Pendleton County representatives have implored the WV Division of Highways to install more safety measures, one of which would be a series of sand pile escape ramps for such runaway trucks. The problem is the width of the road, which has been cut into the side of the mountain and extends to the edge before the land falls away. The only option would be to carve further into the mountain, shuffle the road inward, and leave room for the pits on the outside. The physics are mind boggling and the cost would be well into the millions.

For now, the division is only offering a large retaining wall and rein-forced guardrails around Dead Woman's Curve, the site of fatalities and gruesome vehicular cliff-dives that comes immediately before Horse-shoe Curve, which shares the same appalling statistics.

Locals know the grim reality of Pendleton County travel. A retired state trooper named Rick Gillespie has made it his mission to bring awareness to the dangers of US 33 on Allegheny Mountain. He's been screaming warnings at officials in Charleston since the 1970s. He told me that by the time the trucks reach the top of Allegheny Mountain, their brakes are already overheated from the trip from Elkins, which has no shortage of steep mountain grades. Plus, there are two straight stretches along the descent that fool drivers into thinking they've reached the bottom. Instead, the road whips around into a curve so steep and tight that one mistake can toss the truck off the side of the road, often several hundred feet below. He said when he and the other responders reach a wreck, the scene looks like an airplane crash.

Despite forty years of warnings, protests, and admonitions from West Virginia citizens and local officials, the state has offered no res-olution other than the installation of the mandatory brake check area with a flashing yellow light and a warning sign.

I'd driven this route many times, so I knew there was no way to get to Seneca Shadows Campground, pop-up in tow, without crossing the Allegheny Front. (This is why settlers were forced down into Vir-ginia during their westward expansion centuries ago. It was probably the front's foreboding terrain, but it's possible they never even got to Allegheny Mountain because they were still at camp, jackknifing their Conestoga wagons and backing over wildlife.) I knew what to expect, and this was exactly my problem. I hadn't heard about the deaths, but I'd seen the flashing sign at the top warning truckers to stop, check their brakes, and drive as slowly as they could. I'd seen the insanity of Dead Woman's Curve and Horseshoe Curve and the sheer drop-off the side of the mountain. Now, *I* was going to be towing a trailer. I'd tried to foist the task off on Shawn, but as anyone with anxiety will tell you, the only thing worse than being anxious in the driver's seat is being anxious in the passenger's seat. As my husband would tell you, there's a reason I do all the driving.

"Shawn, you're in the wrong lane."

"There's a backup twelve miles down the road. Better start slowing down now."

"The wipers are going too fast and there's not enough rain on the window and they're leaving rubber smears on the glass and I just bought them and you're going to wear them out and what the fuck you just blew right past our exit."

Thus, he thought it best to let me do the driving. "To face your fears," he said, in the same tone he used when he told me I was "very special" when I got hungry.

I scheduled the camping trip for the first weekend after school let out. And as any Generalized Anxiety Disorder sufferer worth their Zoloft will do, I started worrying in February. *Shit, we're going to have to go down that absurd road.*

I worried in March and installed a trailer brake controller on my car. This electronic device activates the trailer's brakes when the car's brakes engage. It's a smart thing to have, whether or not you're crossing the Allegheny Front.

I worried in April and checked in with my West Virginia camping group to see if I was overreacting. They told me I was. "Just take your time." The same advice my husband had given me. He wasn't worried. Or preoccupied. And he definitely hadn't pictured me tossing the entire family off the side of a cliff like our ginger cat, Beaker, whacking my coffee cup.

I worried in May and combed the maps I already knew by heart, looking for a sneak, a portage around the obstacle. There weren't any good options, so I alternated between telling myself it was all going to be fine and drafting a posthumous document to be read after the great plunge in which I apologized to the first responders, bequeathed my estate to my overweight rescue hound, and humbly asked that a bronze statue of me in a contemplative pose be erected at the county line, but with a stronger chin.

On Thursday, June 3, we double- and triple-checked the camper and its connection to the car. We did a brake light check, a turn signal check. And then, we left the house with two adults, two kids, one West Virginia Brown Dog, a propane tank, two coolers, and enough Oreos to get us through the first few days of any potential apocalyptic events before we started considering who to eat first. (For the record, it's still Andy.)

Shawn drove us south through the center of the state on I-79 for two hours until we reached Buckhannon, where we got off the interstate and he handed me the keys.

"I don't want to," I said.

"You'll be fine," he said. And because he took my seat when I stopped at Sheetz to pee, I didn't have much choice, so eastward I drove. I gripped the steering wheel and cursed at my tiny bladder all the way to Elkins, where we picked up US Route 33 and began to climb into Randolph County's high, wild places. As the road rose steadily, we looked to the north and saw the looming green knobs of Otter Creek Wilderness. We descended again, into the hamlet of Harman, which went by in about thirteen seconds, and then began the Allegheny Front's climb. My stomach narrated the journey with squeaks, whines, and threats of gastrointestinal fisticuffs. By the time we reached the Randolph/Pendleton County line, I thought I might throw up.

At the top of Allegheny Mountain, the familiar yellow sign flashed its cautionary message.

TRUCK WARNING

STEEP GRADE

SHARP CURVES

NEXT 3 ½ MILES

It's not a sign to be taken lightly. Many drivers who find themselves on 33 are unfamiliar with the region, and their GPS has been "helpfully" guiding them along. Others, especially truckers, need to take the shortest possible route. They've trusted their navigation system, so imagine their shock when they crest the divide and find the road beneath them dropping away. I hadn't considered it much until it was my own foot on the brake pedal, my own trailer pushing me downward.

For the record, I knew that by trucking standards, the load behind me was utterly laughable, a mere 2,700 pounds of camper. The veteran drivers in my West Virginia camper group reassured me from one side of their mouths while they no doubt guffawed out the other. In logical moments, I recognized the descent wasn't the deadly tapestry I'd woven in my head. But my guts were careening down a mountain of their own, with my clinical anxiety at the wheel. Shawn told me not to pull over because, if I did, I'd probably bail out, yak on my own shoes, and walk the rest of the way down. So I put the car in a lower gear and began to inch down Dead Woman's Curve.

At first, it wasn't especially intense. I tried not to ride the brake, because of course I'd had nightmares about burning through the brake pads in the first fifteen seconds, something I was told wasn't possible, but I figured if anybody could reach such astounding heights of automotive calamity, it would be me. I shifted into the lowest gear, and the engine responded with its expected growl as our growing inertia carried us into the grip of our seatbelts.

Two motorcycles zipped up behind me. Now I had not only an audience but also one that was antsy to get around me. There was a single descending lane, though, so they had no choice but to apply their own brakes and endure the agonizing creep of the pop-up camper in front of them and what could only be a ninety-two-year-old woman at the wheel. The boys, zoned out in the back with their earbuds in, had no idea how close we were to death. And I always say that when it comes time to die, I'd prefer to do it in the mountains. I stand by that, but I'd like to amend the preference to exclude woodpecker attacks, tainted hot dogs, and, most of all, dramatic vehicular plunges.

As I came out of Dead Woman's Curve and hit the first straightaway, I gained a little speed—just enough to feel both confident about my driving prowess and relatively certain that the brakes were smoking. I asked the kids if they smelled anything. Ben rolled his eyes.

"Great, Mom's got the farts, again."

Next came Horseshoe Curve, named for its distinctive shape. I crept along at a geriatric pace. The motorcyclists buzzed close enough to hop into the camper's beds. The kids munched chips. Shawn commented on a grazing woodchuck. Nobody offered me water or rubbed my back or mopped my brow as we turned east, then north, then east, then south again. A quick straightaway, and the final curve, less intense than the other two and really more of a bend—though still deadly—vanished into the distance.

And then we were done. The car, the camper, and the family puttered down off the mountain.

They say not all heroes wear capes. On June 3, 2021, I was that hero.

"Nice job, Lar," Shawn said. "Let's go find some more Munchos."

*Munchos?* Did the man not realize what I'd just done? I'd kept us alive. I'd kept us on the road, didn't launch us off the side of a mountain. We weren't lying in a smoking heap at the bottom of a cliff. After months of worry, planning, desperate prayer, and, yes, a few nervous farts (it was the dog), I'd done it.

I knew it was a little thing to most people, the tiniest of victories over a silly fear, one to which most drivers probably wouldn't have given an ounce of time or energy. But it meant something to me.

Still, I didn't look at the journey as a victory over the mountain. In classic anxiety-sufferer fashion, I enjoyed my success just long enough to stop, pee (again), buy Munchos, and take a family photo at Seneca Rocks before realizing I had to do it all again, in reverse, in three days—the climb up the escarpment of the Allegheny Front, the topography that repelled settlers, drove them south to find safer routes. The road—and the mountain—would wait for me until I returned, ready to try again.

The Sherpa people, who traditionally work as guides and porters for Himalayan climbing expeditions, tell visitors who have paid tens of thousands of dollars to climb Mount Everest that no one *conquers* Chomolungma, goddess mother of the world. If they make it to the top and survive the journey back down, it's because she has allowed their passage. Before each climb, they do a *puja*, a ritual that honors the deity and asks for her blessing on the expedition. Some climbers receive it. Some do not.

Everest is 50 million years old. Allegheny Mountain is 600 million. And while we can't know which of West Virginia's ancient peaks might once have been the highest, the goddess mother that looked down upon all the other ridges around her, I'm grateful our passage was blessed. The flat earth may be safer, but I'll take my chances here, in her arms.

# Quick Reference Guide

**Allegheny Front:** An escarpment that marks the boundary between the Appalachian Plateau to the west and the Ridge-and-Valley Province to the east. The front once proved a formidable obstacle for settlers moving West. Some traveled in search of water gaps like Blair Gap and Kittanning Gap while others just gave up and went back to the beach.

**Cranberry Wilderness:** Pocahontas and Webster Counties. 47,815 acres of wilderness in the Monongahela National Forest. Named for Cranberry Glades, a boreal bog area above 3,000 feet that resembles a Canadian ecosystem. Two species of carnivorous plants lurk in the bog: the purple pitcher plant and the sundew. However, they're not big enough to take more than a couple of toes, so either skip the flip-flops or bring cocktail weenies to distract them.

**Dolly Sods Wilderness:** 17,776 protected acres atop a high and blustery plateau in Tucker, Randolph, and Grant counties. Like Cranberry Wilderness, the climate is reminiscent of Canada. The Sods is a delicate ecosystem struggling with increasing numbers of visitors and was also used in the 1940s for World War II training exercises. Signs warn hikers not to pick up any artillery or mortar shells they find because Americans apparently need to be discouraged from pocketing live explosives.

**Greenbrier River:** 162-mile river in southeastern West Virginia. One of the state's most beautiful and longest rivers, the Greenbrier flows into the New River, which flows into the Kanawha River, which flows into the Ohio River, which flows into the Mississippi River, which flows into the Gulf of Mexico. I'm not sure what happens after that, but if anyone sees my missing sunglasses wash up on Fort Myers Beach, please send them back. They're bifocals.

**Marshall County:** The northern panhandle's southernmost county. Known for the ominous and brutal former West Virginia Penitentiary and the seventy-foot tall Grave Creek Mound, one of the largest such burial sites built by the Adena people roughly three thousand years ago. Marshall County residents have included Brad Paisley, Charles Manson, and Lady Gaga's grandparents.

**Mystery Hole:** Famous tourist trap in Fayette County, located near the New River Gorge National Park and Hawks Nest State Park. Self-proclaimed "best kept secret in West Virginia." While the Hole's website offers only vague clues as to what lies within the ramshackle tin building, sources report it's a gravity room. Those with heart conditions, seizures, and vertigo should skip this one, as should anybody who's consumed more than one West Virginia Hot Dog within the previous hour.

**Pendleton County:** If the eastern part of West Virginia is an arm, Pendleton is the tip of the elbow. I haven't talked with everybody else about that though, so it's still an unofficial designation. Pendleton is known for tall places like Seneca Rocks, Spruce Knob, and North Fork Mountain; deep places like Smoke Hole and Seneca Caverns; and foody places like the Gateway Restaurant. Get the pie.

**Ridge-and-Valley Province:** Also known as the Ridge-and-Valley Appalachians. Named for a series of long, even ridges and continuous valleys, this mountain region stretches from Alabama to New York and is sandwiched between the Allegheny Plateau and the Blue Ridge Mountains. Some ridges in West Virginia include North Fork Mountain, Sleepy Creek Mountain, The Robert C. Byrd Big-Ass Rock Pile, and a hill we just call Kevin.

**Spruce Knob:** West Virginia's highest mountain, elevation 4,863 feet. Located in Pendleton County. The Whispering Pines trail at the top leads to an overlook tower that offers sweeping views of the Allegheny Front and Ridge-and-Valley Province. Visitors can explore a forest of flagged red spruce, a talus field of 300-million-year-old Pennsylvania Pottsfield sandstone boulders, and a pit toilet reported to have consumed three cell phones, five sets of earbuds, and my Southwest Airlines Rapid Rewards Visa card.

**Spruce Knob Lake:** Remote man-made lake and nearby campground. The lake is stocked with trout, but those seeking its alpine waters should prepare for several miles of potholes en route. Popular with astral photographers seeking the darkest place in the eastern US. No motors are allowed on the lake, but you can make the *b-b-b-b-b-b-b* noise with your lips while you paddle.

**Wheeling:** Ohio County seat. Following the Wheeling Conventions of 1861, West Virginia bid farewell to the Confederacy and declared itself a state in 1863. However, the capital couldn't sit still and moved to Charleston in 1870. Still antsy, it came back to Wheeling in 1875, and we got really excited here until it dumped us *again* and went back to Charleston in 1885. My hometown of Wheeling is known for Oglebay Park, Coleman's fish sandwiches, and orange traffic cones.

**New River Gorge:** That place where they throw people off that bridge.

——THINGS

**Derecho of June 29, 2012:** This exceptionally strong storm, driven by eighty-mile-per-hour, straightline winds blasted through West Virginia and left 670,000 people in the dark for up to two weeks during a dangerous heat spell. The outages were so widespread that many hotels were also out of commission, so we did what West Virginians do best: sucked it up, hunkered down, and talked about how long we might have to suck it up and hunker down.

**Flatwoods Monster:** aka the Braxton County Monster or "Braxie." First sighted in 1952 in the town of Flatwoods. On an early September night, three boys spotted a bright light in the sky. They gathered a small group and went in search of the source, which turned out to be a tall creature with a red face and a green cape and hood. The being, surrounded by a reeking fog, hissed at the group, who ran for the hollows, fainting and vomiting as they went. Since then, Braxie has become one of West

Virginia's most famous monsters, and cryptid hunters come from all over the country hoping for their own thrilling chance to run, faint, and vomit.

**Giant Teapot:** The world's largest teapot sits in Chester, at the top of the northern panhandle. The fourteen-by-fourteen-foot behemoth arrived in Hancock County in 1938 after retiring from its first job as a barrel-shaped Hires Root Beer sign. Fun teapot fact: One of its owners invented the banana split in nearby Latrobe, Pennsylvania, in 1904. Not so fun teapot fact: Yeah, right. There aren't any. Everything about teapots is fun.

**Hellbender:** aka Snot Otter, Allegheny Alligator, and Old Lasagna Sides. North America's largest salamander, found in some West Virginia streams and rivers. Hellbenders are dark, slippery, and wrinkly. Habitat includes the protected Monongahela National Forest. Hellbenders have a fifty to seventy-year lifespan and live under rocks on the river bottom, where they're vulnerable to the effects of habitat loss, pollution, and sedimentation. Movement of river rocks—including stacking them for photos—can crush hellbenders living beneath. So don't be that guy who stacks rocks. Instagram is sick of your shit, anyway.

**Hollow:** Also known as a *holler*. West Virginia is made up of two things: hills and hollows. These narrow valleys are carved by streams and thickly wooded. Governor Jim Justice once mentioned Raleigh County's "Hoohoo Holler" in one of his interviews. I haven't seen the place with my own eyes, but according to some lady on the internet, her brother-in-law Stew lives there. He's going to be selling his ATV, and apparently, he's open to interesting trades.

**Lightning Bug:** When it comes to *lightning bugs* versus *fireflies*—two names for the same sweet beetles—West Virginians are Team Lightning Bug. We tolerate Team Firefly, but it's an uneasy truce, and we're not opposed to fisticuffs in the parking lot.

**Mothman:** West Virginia has been blessed/cursed with a robust population of cryptids, including the Flatwoods Monster, the Grafton Monster,

Sheepsquatch, Bat Boy, the Snallygaster, the Snarly Yow, and the most beloved of all: Mothman. The winged, screeching, red-eyed creature was first seen in Point Pleasant in 1966 and reportedly hung around for a full month, terrorizing locals and peering in windows. Mothman's visit to Point Pleasant ended when the Silver Bridge, which connected the town with Gallipolis, Ohio, collapsed into the river, killing forty-six. Some say Mothman was an omen of the disaster to come; biologists say Mothman was likely a sandhill crane. Today, a stainless steel statue of the pantsless cryptid casts its ruby gaze toward Main Street in downtown Point Pleasant, where you can grab a coffee, visit the Mothman Museum, and run your hands over the gleaming silver hams of West Virginia's legendary "shiny hiney."

**Mountain Dew:** Stereotypes hold that West Virginians' choice beverage is the hundred-proof, liver-searing elixir of life we call moonshine. And don't get me wrong—we start each day with a hearty mug of it, baptize our children in it, and would gladly fill our waterbeds with White Lightning if it wouldn't eat through the mattress liner in eleven minutes. But in truth, the highly caffeinated, heavily sugared, yellow demon fizz known as Mountain Dew is the real addiction for many Appalachians. And while the farm-to-table movement rises and more organic options appear, "Mountain Dew mouth" remains a problem for the all-day sippers and slurpers of this unholy concoction. We know—it's a bad look. Also, who the hell thought waterbeds were a brilliant idea?

**Pawpaw:** *Asimina triloba*, the American pawpaw tree. Roughly the size of a hamster, pawpaws are the largest edible fruit native to the US. The texture is custard-like; the taste is somewhere between banana, pineapple, and mango. Pawpaws ripen in the fall, and many West Virginians collect them to be eaten raw or made into beer or ice cream or baked goods. I have yet to experience the beverage or the frozen wonder of pawpaw ice cream, but I can confirm that while pawpaw quick bread may delight the taste buds and warm the heart, for some unlucky souls, the baked or dehydrated fruit—petite though it be—can also trigger a Tunguska-level bout of GI distress.

**Pepperoni Roll:** The food of our people. When young West Virginians leave the state for the first time, they're often shocked to learn the rest of the world has no idea what a pepperoni roll is. First created in Fairmont in 1927, these baked balls of soft bread, cheese, and pepperoni (sometimes a stick, sometimes slices—people fight about this so choose a side carefully) do not need to be refrigerated and originally made a quick and hearty lunch for coal miners. Every meat-eating West Virginian will have a favorite pepperoni roll source, and they're usually gas stations. My dad likes the one on Route 88 south in Ohio County.

**"West-by-God Virginia":** While the exact date and origin of this phrase is unknown, it may have begun as an expression of indignancy, e.g., "We're not Virginians! We're West-by-God Virginians!" It's a useful phrase. Sometimes we exclaim it. Sometimes we spit it. Most often, we toss it out with pride. Once, in St. Petersburg, Florida, the cashier in lane five at the 54th Avenue South Alberton's supermarket asked for my license, then broke into a smile and said, "Well! West *by God* Virginia!" After four minutes, he asked me to stop hugging him, but it took me another seven to stop crying.

**West Virginia Hot Dog:** Like the pepperoni roll, the hot dog historically satisfied anyone with a short, standing-only lunch break, a need for protein to sustain their body through manual labor (like digging for coal), and limited funds. Topped with onions, mustard, coleslaw, and "sauce," which is chili sans beans. But don't ask for slaw in Marion County. According to The West Virginia Hot Dog Blog author Stanton Means, Marion County is the "center of the anti-slaw resistance." So far, the movement hasn't spread past the county borders, though rumors of unrest among disgruntled cabbage growers suggest a potential uprising is not inconceivable.

**Wild, Wonderful:** This descriptive and lyrical slogan came into popularity in the 1970s. You'll see it on state line welcome signs, T-shirts, and license plates. For a time, Governor Joe Manchin changed the slogan on the welcome signs to "Open for Business," and we, as a state, absolutely hated it. We complained so loudly that Manchin's office held a public vote. "Wild, Wonderful" won in a landslide and became the official state slogan in 2007. Recently, I noticed that newer license plates do not have the comma between "wild" and "wonderful." The DMV refuses to comment on this, and Peggy in my local office strongly urged me to abandon any further grammatical investigations into this matter. She looked scared.

——A WORD ON PRONUNCIATION . . .
Don't feel badly if you get corrected by a West Virginian in conversation. We've been determined since the beginning to mangle as many proper nouns as possible. This is by no means an exhaustive list but should get you through a drive around the state. I'd suggest checking the internet for information when you arrive in a new town, but you probably won't have cell service anyway.

**Cairo:** *KAY-roh*
**Canaan:** *ka-NAYNE*
**Chelyan:** *SHEEL-yun*
**Erbacon:** *UR-bake-uh*
**Ghent:** *Jent*
**Hepzibah, in Harrison County:** *HEP-zee-bah*
**Hepzibah, in adjacent Taylor County:** *HEP-zee-bee*
**Hurricane:** *HURR-i-kin*
**Kanawha:** *kuh-NAW*
**Kumbrabow:** *kum-BRAY-bow*
**Philippi:** *PHIL-i-pee*
**Onego:** *ONE-go*
**Rio:** *RYE-oh*

# Gratitude & Acknowledgments

My heartfelt thanks to the publishers who took a chance on the following essays, which were published under the name Laura Jackson Roberts:
"To Catch a Craw," *Still: The Journal*
"Country Roads: A Brief Primer," *Dead Skunk*
"Oh, Possum," *Terrain.org*
"The West Virginia Brown Dog," *Heartwood*
"Pure, Unadulterated Garbage," originally published as "Coyotes: Truth, Myth & What We're Getting Wrong" by *Weelunk*
"Intruder Alert," originally published as "West Virginia's Remarkable Bats" and "Roberts Ruminates: Intruder Alert" by *Weelunk*
"Snagging a Spot for Stumpy," originally published as "Valley Views & Varmints: Snagging a Spot for Stumpy" by *Weelunk*

My utmost gratitude to the 2023 Autumn House contest judge Jenny Boully, as well, for seeing something in these essays and for putting this book on the top of the pile. Thank you for your belief and trust.

Ten years ago, I had thoughts and feelings and an overwhelming love for this deep and wild place . . . and a ferocious desire to share them. Now, you're holding them in your hands. And you wouldn't be if not for the people with whom I've walked and, in many cases, been led, through forests, mountains, and this beautiful, literary life.

I wrote my first humorous story in fourth grade. Since then, I've been lucky enough to have teachers who pushed me, believed in me, kicked me in the butt when warranted, and showed me such kindness and encouragement. None ever seemed to doubt me, even when I doubted myself and them and all that I had learned. Perhaps this is the true mark of a teacher.

With that in mind, I'd like to thank:

Mary Ann Galbreath, Cassie Edwards, Rob Hunter, Robin Follet, David Mallow, Rich Wallace, Sheila Squillante, Kate Miles, Suzanne

Roberts, Tim "Bean" Parrish, Mel Fox, Lori Jakiela, Paul Hertneky, Dinty W. Moore, and Allison Williams . . . thank you for your guidance, your advice, and your support.

And just as writers must have guides, so must we also have other writers on our journey. I met my literary family at Chatham University, and a decade later, these smart, talented women continue to support me despite bad metaphors, vague language, jokes that don't land, ridiculous titles, and frequent what-have-I-done-with-my-life emergency texts. To my Bitter Lit Hags—Maria Brisbane, Lainy Carslaw, Amanda Jaros, and Kim Hambright Michalak—thank you for your eyes, your words, your ears, and your hearts. I'm grateful for you every day.

I'd also like to acknowledge:

All of my sources, including the late Rich Rogers, the late Ben Stout, Kathy Kyle, Dr. Shelden Owen, Rick Gillespie, Stan Lake, and the Road Home Animal Project (which has brought so many West Virginia Brown Dogs like Minnie into loving homes).

The wonderful folks at Autumn House: Christine Stroud, for her belief, support, and enthusiasm; and Mike Good, my kind-hearted, patient editor, who offered grace and encouragement through forty-five title changes, thirty-seven attacks of impostor syndrome, and four existential crises.

Simmons Buntin at *Terrain.org*, who took a liking to Eugene the opossum years ago, who has nominated the stinky critter for awards, and who never failed to offer his support and congratulations.

Marc Harshman, who's always around, cheering for me and telling the story of Appalachia in words we're so very lucky to hear. It's an honor to call you a friend.

Phyllis Sigal, Empress of Puns and my first editor. You let me run wild and write about whatever I wanted. And you took a little Wheeling blog and turned it into a tapestry of stories, history and art. Please note that I didn't use an Oxford comma in the previous sentence. I hated it, but I did it for you.

Christina Fisanick, the funniest, kindest, most loyal friend, and a gifted writer. You're the Dale to my Chip, the cat to my dog. You've wiped my tears at two o'clock in the morning, raised many a glass with me, and never, ever failed to show up when I needed you. Thanks for staying close and for so elevating the words of northern Appalachian writers.

Janelle Friedline, to whom I've whispered every secret, who once ran with me through a haunted cornfield from a man with a chainsaw, who squeezed my hand when my newborn got rabies shots, who has been the first person I've spoken to each morning for the last twenty years and the first person I hope to speak to each morning for the next forty. I'm so deeply grateful for you, every day.

Caroline Hinchliff and my brother, David. Thank you for your love, your support, your belief, and every step you've taken with me and my kids through so many remarkable landscapes and experiences. You've always had my back, and you've always been ready for an adventure. We have many more to come.

Shawn. Thank you for following me all over this green earth. You gave me room to grow and pushed me along, gently enough that I didn't always notice. You knew I was a writer before I did, and you've taught our sons to be the kind of people who will soften hearts and change the world around them. I'm grateful for every mile we traveled together, for the destinations, and the journeys.

Andy and Ben. Thank you for always going on Mom-hikes, even if you did so to be nice; for popping a Dramamine on country roads so we could find "just one more waterfall" and see "just one more scenic view"; for singing "Country Roads" with me like Siberian huskies; for your wonderful curiosity about the world and the ideas with which you're filling it; and for your patience and joy as we wandered into forests, up mountains, through deserts, and down rivers. You're the kindest people I've ever known, and the world is going to need that, and you. I'm so proud to be your mom.

Brad Mills. When I found you, I found me. Thank you for making me laugh, endlessly. Thank you for understanding why I run through the woods like a wild woman and for always knowing what I mean, no matter how boingy and incoherent I get. Thank you for teaching me to trust the Universe, and for walking, writing, and napping beside me. Everyone needs a huckleberry; I am so grateful you are mine.

My parents. Parents shape us into the people we become. Their magnetic influence pulls us along the path, the one where they help us stand, for the first time. If we're lucky, they walk with us, and mine have. So much of this book came from my father, who took me to deep and wild places before I could walk. He taught me to love mountains, to paddle rivers, to listen to ice, to find the moon, to never miss a sunset, and to return to the woods, season after season. We've hiked a thousand Sunday miles with a pack of West Virginia Brown Dogs, and I've loved every step. Thanks, Dad.

My mom's influence came not from wild adventures but from her constant, quiet presence, one so very strong, and one in which I've felt loved, every day. She devoted her life to me when I was born, a selfless choice made because she never wanted to miss a day of my life. And she hasn't. I never questioned whether she would be there for me . . . because she's never left my side. I love you, Mom. I couldn't ask for more.

# NEW & FORTHCOMING FROM AUTUMN HOUSE PRESS

*Book of Kin* by Darius Atefat-Peckham
Winner of the 2023 Autumn House Poetry Prize, selected by January Gill O'Neil

*Near Strangers* by Marian Crotty
Winner of the 2023 Autumn House Fiction Prize, selected by Pam Houston

*Deep & Wild: On Mountains, Opossums & Finding Your Way in West Virginia* by Laura Jackson
Winner of the 2023 Autumn House Nonfiction Prize, selected by Jenny Boully

*Terminal Maladies* by Okwudili Nebeolisa
Winner of the 2023 CAAPP Book Prize, selected by Nicole Sealey

*I Have Not Considered Consequences: Short Stories* by Sherrie Flick

*The Worried Well* by Anthony Immergluck
Winner of the 2024 Rising Writer Prize, selected by Eduardo C. Corral

*Rodeo* by Sunni Brown Wilkinson
Winner of the 2024 Donald Justice Poetry Prize, selected by Patricia Smith

**For our full catalog please visit autumnhouse.org**